Formal Specification
Using Z

Second Edition

Formal Specification Using Z

Second Edition

David Lightfoot

palgrave

© David Lightfoot 2001

First published 2001 by
PALGRAVE
Houndmills, Basingstoke, Hampshire RG21 6XS and
175 Fifth Avenue, New York, N.Y. 10010
Companies and representatives throughout the world

PALGRAVE is the new global academic imprint of
St. Martin's Press LLC Scholarly and Reference Division and
Palgrave Publishers Ltd (formerly Macmillan Press Ltd).

ISBN 0–333–76327–0 paperback

This book is printed on paper suitable for recycling and
made from fully managed and sustained forest sources.

A catalogue record for this book is available
from the British Library.

10   9   8   7   6   5   4   3   2
10   09   08   07   06   05   04   03   02

Printed in Great Britain by
Antony Rowe Ltd, Chippenham and Eastbourne

Contents

Contents

Contents

Preface to the Second Edition

In the years that have passed since the original appearance of this book, my contention, expressed in the original preface, that many can benefit from the study of formal specification, has been borne out many times. Large numbers of students in my own university and elsewhere in the United Kingdom and the rest of Europe have discovered that the mathematics involved is *not* beyond their grasp, when suitably presented, and that the study of formal specification helps clarify their ideas in diverse areas of computing and software engineering.

The Z notation has evolved over that time and this second edition takes that into account. New examples and exercises have been included and sections rewritten in the light of experience.

I am grateful to the many students, in Britain and France in particular, who have given me feedback; to colleagues who have provided careful help, and to my publishers, who have provided patient encouragement and help.

The aims of this book

This book aims to help readers learn about formal specification using the Z language. I believe that formal specification offers substantial benefits to the developers of computer systems and will make a major contribution towards improving their quality.

I further believe that if it is to make such contributions it must be used widely and not just by those with proven mathematical ability. Experience of teaching students who do not consider themselves mathematicians has convinced me that this is possible. Even if they do not use what they have learned immediately, the mathematical concepts of formal specification seem to help clarify thinking by providing a language for discussing the behaviour of computer systems.

The scope of this book

This book aims to cover the main ideas of formal specification in Z in a style that will be accessible to the reader who is not very familiar with mathematics. To achieve this, the explanations have been kept somewhat informal and certain aspects of the notation have been given less emphasis than others or are even omitted.

How to use this book

The chapters of this book contain explanations of the mathematics of Z, interleaved with the development of an example specification. The chapters covering mathematics finish with a summary of the notation introduced in the chapter and a set of exercises. Sample solutions to selected exercises are included in Appendix 2.

Acknowledgements

I am grateful to the members of the Programming Research Group of Oxford University, firstly for their pioneering work on Z and secondly for teaching it to me when I studied there for an MSc. What I have learned about Z is largely due to them, but I alone am responsible for any errors in this book.

I am also grateful to my then employer and colleagues for their assistance in making it possible for me to learn.

David Lightfoot, Oxford 2000

Introduction

1.1 Who this book is for

The word 'formal' in 'formal specification' means *mathematical*. Many practitioners and students of software engineering do not think of themselves as mathematicians and may not make use of mathematics in their work. Nonetheless, there are many ways in which the appropriate use of mathematics can aid in such work.

This book is intended for the practitioner or student who wishes to learn about formal specification in a gentle and straightforward manner. All the necessary mathematical concepts are introduced, with examples chosen to reflect everyday experience rather than technical areas. The mathematics used does *not* include: differentiation, quadratic equations, integration, trigonometry or transcendental functions; instead, it is based on discrete mathematics: the arithmetic of whole numbers, set theory and simple logic.

Even those who do not anticipate ever using formal specification in their work, or further study, will find that the concepts, specialised vocabulary and need for precision that they acquire through a study of formal specification will enrich their thinking and means of expression in all aspects of software engineering. This has been the experience of the countless students both in the United Kingdom and elsewhere who have studied this area, many by using this book.

An early review of this book described it as a 'lightweight' introduction. But that was not to be taken as a criticism, since that is precisely what the book sets out to be.

1.2 The need for formal specification

1.2.1 Problems in the creation of computer systems

There are long-standing problems in the development of computer systems: often they take too much time to produce, cost more than estimated and fail to satisfy the customer. This 'software crisis' was first identified in the 1960s and has been the subject of much research and controversy, and it is still not entirely solved.

Central to the problem is the fact that errors and inadequacies are more expensive to correct the later in the development process they are discovered. Furthermore, it is extremely difficult to clarify exactly what is required of a very complex system.

1.2.2 Software Engineering

A variety of techniques have been introduced to help deal with the difficulties of developing computer systems. These techniques are moving towards the concept of *software engineering*, where well established principles of the engineering professions are being applied to the creation of software systems. Amongst these principles is the idea that appropriate mathematical techniques should be applied in the analysis and solution of engineering problems.

1.2.3 Formal Methods

Techniques which use mathematical principles to develop computer systems are collectively known as *formal methods*. The idea of specifying what a computer system is required to do using a mathematical notation and techniques of mathematical manipulation, has led to notations for *formal specification*.

1.3 The role of mathematics

1.3.1 Background of mathematics

Mathematics has a very long history, spanning thousands of years of work by mathematicians in many different civilisations. The major principles of mathematics are now stable and proven in use in scientific and engineering applications. It is therefore appropriate to apply these to the development of computer systems.

1.3.2 Precision

Mathematical expressions have the advantage of being *precise* and *unambiguous*. There will never be any need for discussion or confusion regarding what a formal specification *means*.

1.3.3 Conciseness

Mathematical expressions are typically very concise; a great deal of meaning is concentrated in a relatively small number of symbols. This is a particular advantage when describing a very complex system.

1.3.4   Abstraction

The mathematical notion of *abstraction* plays an important role in formal methods. Abstraction involves initially considering only the essential issues of a problem and deferring consideration of all other aspects until a later stage. This *separation of concerns* is the best way of coping with the complexity of large systems.

1.3.5   Independence from natural language

The independence of mathematical forms from the context of spoken (natural) language means that mathematics can be equally well understood by all readers – irrespective of their language and culture.

1.3.6   Proofs

Deductions and conclusions expressed in a mathematical form are capable of being *proved*, by application of established mathematical laws. The ability to prove such things, rather than just to demonstrate them, or convince oneself informally of their validity, is an important aspect of the application of mathematics. This is particularly so when the consequences of an invalid conclusion could endanger life, in so-called *safety-critical* systems.

1.4   Current use of mathematics

Many practitioners involved with the development of computer systems are not mathematicians and do not make regular use of mathematics in their work. However, mathematical techniques are assuming an increasingly important role in the development of computer systems and it is appropriate that they should be known and applied by as many practitioners as possible.

1.4.1   Discrete mathematics

The mathematics used in formal specification is very simple. It is called *discrete mathematics* and is concerned more with sets and logic than with numbers. This means that even those who have studied mathematics before will probably have something new to learn. Conversely, those who have not previously been very successful at learning mathematics have a new area of mathematics to study and have the motivating factor that the benefits will be immediately applicable to their work.

In this book, all the necessary mathematical notations are introduced, with examples. Where necessary, a conventional or possible pronunciation is given. This can aid understanding and is also vital if people are to talk to each other about mathematics. However, the introductory mathematical parts are deliberately kept brief and in some places informal, since the topic of the book is the *application* of the mathematics.

1.5 The specification language Z

1.5.1 Background

The specification language Z (pronounced 'zed' in Great Britain) was initiated by Jean-Raymond Abrial in France and developed by a team at the Programming Research Group (PRG) of Oxford University in England, led by Professor C. A. R. Hoare. It is foremost amongst specification notations in use at present.

Z is used to specify new computer systems and to describe the behaviour of existing complex computer systems.

It is increasingly being learned by both practitioners of software engineering and by students. The aim of this book is to help in that process.

A Z specification works by modelling the *states* that a system can take, the *operations* that causes changes in those states to take place and the *enquiries* that can discover information about those states.

1.5.2 Software tools

The Z notation uses a set of characters, many of which are not found on most typewriter or computer keyboards. Most of the extra characters are widely used mathematical symbols, but some are new and confined to Z.

In general, Z text cannot be prepared using conventional typewriting equipment and several *software tools* have been created to permit the typesetting of text written in Z. Some of these software tools also check the text to make sure that it conforms to the rules of the Z notation (its *syntax*).

Other software tools are concerned with giving automated assistance to the process of creating mathematical proofs. Some of these are called *theorem provers* and attempt the entire proof without manual intervention; others, called *proof assistants*, support the human activity of creating proofs.

1.6 Textual aspects of the Z notation

The Z notation is used in *specification documents* which consist of sections written in Z interleaved with narrative text in natural language. Z also uses a graphical device called the *schema*, which is a box containing the mathematics. As well as having a useful effect in visually separating the mathematics from the narrative, schemas have important special properties which will be explained in this book.

1.6.1   Identifiers

There is a need to invent names when creating a formal specification. The rules for constructing such *identifiers* are similar to those of computer programming languages.

> ▹ Identifiers may be any length and are constructed from the (upper- and lower-case) Roman letters without diacriticals marks (accents, umlauts, etc.) and from the numeric digits and the 'low-line' ('underscore') character ('_').

> ▹ The first character must be a letter.

> ▹ The upper-case and lower-case letters are considered to be different.

> ▹ Only a single word may be used for an identifier; when this needs to be a compound of several words the *low-line* character (_) can be used, or the convention of starting each component of the identifier with an upper-case letter can be adopted. For example:
>
>   very_long_identifier
>   VeryLongIdentifier

> ▹ By convention, identifiers of variables start with a lower-case letter, identifiers of types are written entirely in capital letters, and identifiers of *schemas* begin with a capital letter.

> ▹ The special characters Δ and Ξ on the front of an identifier, and ? and ! and ' on the end, have special meanings that will be explained later.

EXERCISES

1. An annual weekend event begins on the Friday evening and finishes on the Sunday afternoon. The date of the event is specified as: 'the last weekend in September'. What is the date of the Friday on which the event begins if the last day of September (30th) in that year is:
    (a) a Monday;
    (b) a Sunday;
    (c) a Saturday;
    (d) a Friday?
       Suggest an unambiguous specification of the date of the event.

2. On Friday the first of the month a software engineer goes away leaving an undated message on her/his desk saying: 'Software engineer on leave until next Wednesday'. A colleague from another department passes the desk on Monday 4th of the same month and

reads the message. When would the colleague expect the software engineer next to be back at work?

3.   A video cassette recorder has a 'programming' facility which allows recordings to be made in the user's absence. Requests for recordings consist of: start-date, start-time, end-time and channel-number. Dates are specified by month-number and day-number. Times are given as hours and minutes using the 24-hour clock. If the end-time is earlier in the day than the start-time then the end-time is considered to be on the following day. Up to eight requests can be stored and are numbered one to eight.

How would you expect the recorder to behave in the following circumstances?

(a)   start-date does not exist, for example, 31st April.

(b)   start-date does not exist; not a leap year, 29 February.

(c)   start- and end-times for different requests overlap (on same day).

(d)   start-date is for New Year's Eve and end-time is earlier in the day than start-time.

(e)   requests are not in chronological order. For example, request 1 is for a recording which occurs later than that of request 2.

Look at the user handbook for a video cassette recorder similar to the one described here. Does the handbook answer these questions?

4.   In the requirements specification of a computer program it is stated that: 'The records input to the program should be sorted in order of increasing key.'

Does this mean that the program may be written on the assumption that the records will already have been sorted (by some external agent), or does it mean that the program must perform the required sorting?

5.   Look at the manual(s) for any reasonably complex machine or system. Find the parts which are ambiguous or unclear and pose questions that are reasonable to ask but which are not answered by the manual.

Sets

2.1 Types

A *set* is a collection of components called *elements* or *members*. The Z notation uses *typed* set theory: all the possible values of a set are considered to have something in common, and are said to have the same *type*. For example, we will have sets of *persons*, or sets of *numbers*, but not just sets that can contain *any* sort of element. Any set is therefore considered to be a *subset* of its type. A *subset* is any collection of values from a set. For example, the even numbers are a subset of the integer numbers.

The notion of type helps in two ways:

▶ it avoids certain mathematical paradoxes;

▶ it allows checks to be made that statements about sets make sense.

The checks can be automated by means of computer *software tools* which check the consistency of the mathematical text in a Z document in the same sort of way that a spelling and grammar checker checks the consistency of a document in a natural language.

2.2 The built-in type Integer

The built-in type *integer* can be used in any Z document without the need to introduce it explicitly. It is designated by the symbol

$$\mathbb{Z}$$

and consists of the whole numbers

$$\ldots, -3, -2, -1, 0, 1, 2, 3, \ldots$$

The symbol is sometimes hand-written 'ZZ' and it is pronounced 'integer' or 'zed-zed' or 'fat Z'. It is an example of an *infinite* set.

2.2.1 The standard set Natural

Often, when specifying, we know that a number can never be negative. (For example, someone's age, or the number of elements in a set). To highlight this we can indicate that it is a *natural* number. The *set natural* is a standard subset of the *type* integer that adds the constraint that the value must always be non-negative. Because it is so useful it has a standard designation:

$\mathbb{N}$

It is pronounced 'natural' or 'en-en' or 'fat N'.

In some mathematical contexts the natural numbers are not considered to include zero. The set of natural numbers *excluding zero* can be written as follows:

$\mathbb{N}_1$

2.2.2 Operations on integers

The following operators are defined for the type integer and its subsets:

+	addition
–	subtraction
*	multiplication
div	(integer) division
mod	modulus (remainder after division)

Examples

23 div 5 = 4
23 mod 5 = 3

The normal rules of precedence between operators hold. For example:

5 + 4 * 3 is the same as 5 + (4 * 3)

because the operators *, *div* and *mod* have *higher precedence* (which means that they bind more tightly) than + and –.

2.2.3 Numerical relations

The following relational operators are applicable to integers:

=	equal to
≠	not equal to
<	less than
≤	less than or equal to
>	greater than
≥	greater than or equal to

Note the following:

x = y is the opposite of x ≠ y
x < y is the opposite of x ≥ y
x ≤ y is the opposite of x > y
x > y is the opposite of x ≤ y
x ≥ y is the opposite of x < y

2.3 Basic types

Basic types are also called *given types*. The basic types of a specification are declared without concern for how their actual elements are to be represented. For example, a specification might refer to the set of all possible car registrations without considering how such registrations are represented as characters. A basic type is declared by writing its name in square brackets, with a comment to indicate its intended meaning. The set of car registrations might be called *REGISTRATION* and written:

    [REGISTRATION]   the set of all possible car registrations

By convention, the name of a basic type is written entirely in capital letters and a singular noun is used.

Another basic type might be the set of all persons:

    [PERSON]   the set of all persons

Several types can be given in one line:

    [REGISTRATION, PERSON]

In general, basic types should be chosen to be as widely encompassing as possible. Furthermore, it should be assumed that the elements of the type are uniquely identifiable.

2.4 Free types

Sometimes it is convenient to introduce a type by listing the identifiers of its elements. This can be done with a *free type*. The general format is:

    freeType ::= element$_1$ | element$_2$ | ... | element$_n$

Examples

    RESPONSE ::= yes | no
    STATUS ::= inUse | free | onHold | outOfOrder

2.5 Declaring variables

Each variable name designating a value must be declared. That means it must be introduced and the type of value it refers to must be stated. For example, to introduce a variable *chauffeur* to be of the basic type *PERSON* we write:

    chauffeur: PERSON

This can be pronounced '*chauffeur* is one of the set of values *PERSON*' or '*chauffeur* is drawn from the set *PERSON*' or '*chauffeur* is a *PERSON*'.

In the following examples elements will be drawn from the set *EU*, the set of all countries in the European Union. To allow for membership to change we should declare this as a *basic* type, but we declare it as a free type here for the sake of illustration since it contains only fifteen members, and for the convenience of identifying the elements by their international car registration letters:

Austria	A	Ireland	IRL
Belgium	B	Italy	I
Denmark	DK	Luxembourg	L
France	F	Netherlands	NL
Finland	SF	Portugal	P
Germany	D	Spain	E
Great Britain	GB	Sweden	S
Greece	GR		

EU ::= A | B | DK | F | SF | D | GB | GR | IRL | I | L | NL | P | E | S
the set of countries currently in the European Union

2.6 Single value from a type

To introduce a *variable* called *homeland* which can refer to *one* country in the European Union we would write:

homeland: EU

2.7 Set values

The value of a set can be written by listing its values within *braces* ('curly brackets'):

benelux = {B, NL, L}

The order in which the elements appear does not matter:

{B, NL, L} = {NL, B, L} = { L, B, NL} = {B, L, NL} = {NL, L, B} = {L, NL, B}

Repeating a value does not matter; although it may appear in the list of values several times it can only occur in a *set* only once:

{B, NL, L, NL} = {B, NL, L}

2.8 The empty set

It is possible to have a set with no values; it is called the *empty set*:

Ø

The empty set can also be written as empty braces:

{ }

2.9   Singleton set

A set that contains only one element is called a *singleton* set. For example:

{GB}

Note that a set containing a single element has different type from the element itself: {*GB*} does not have the same type as *GB*. {*GB*} is the *set* of countries containing just Great Britain, but *GB* is a country, not a set.

2.10   Ranges of integers

The range of values

m .. n

where *m* and *n* are integers, stands for the set of integers *m* to *n* inclusive. Note that if

m > n

then

m .. n = Ø

Examples

3 .. 5 = {3, 4, 5}
2 .. 2 = {2}
3 .. 2 = Ø

2.11   Operators

2.11.1   Equivalence

Two values of the same type can be tested to see if they are the same by using the equals sign, as in

x = y

Two sets are equal if they contain exactly the same elements.

Example

{B, NL, L} = {NL, B, L}   these sets contain the same elements

2.11.2   Non-equivalence

Similarly, two values of the same type can be tested to see if they are *not* the same by using the not-equals sign, as in

x ≠ y

Two sets are not-equal if they do not contain exactly the same elements.

Example

> {B, NL} ≠ {B, NL, L} these sets contain different elements

2.11.3 Membership

The *membership* operator is written:

$$\in$$

and is pronounced 'is an element of' or 'is a member of'. The expression involving it is true if the value is an element (member) of the set and false otherwise.

Example

> NL ∈ {B, NL, L}   this is true; the Netherlands is in 'Benelux'

('Benelux' is a name sometimes used for the group of European countries consisting of Belgium, the Netherlands and Luxembourg.)

The diagrams in this chapter used to illustrate the set operators are called *Venn* diagrams. Figure 2.1 shows the set S, a subset of some type X. The element x of type X is a member of the set S:

Figure 2.1

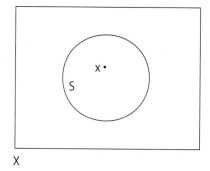

[X]

S: ℙ X

x: X

x ∈ S

2.11.4 Non-membership

The *non-membership* operator is written

$$\notin$$

and is pronounced 'is not an element of' or 'is not a member of'. The expression involving it is true if the value is *not* an element (member) of the set and false otherwise.

Example

> GB ∉ {B, NL, L}   this is true; GB is not a member of Benelux

Figure 2.2 shows the set S, a subset of some type X. The element x of type X is *not* a member of the set S:

Figure 2.2

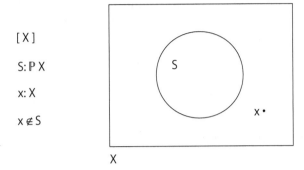

[X]

S: ℙ X

x: X

x ∉ S

X

2.11.5 Validity of membership test

Note that the value to be tested for membership must be an element of the underlying type of the set. For example, the expression:

USA ∈ {B, NL, L}

is neither true nor false but *illegal*, since *USA* is not an element of the type *EU*.

2.11.6 Size, cardinality

The number of values in a set is called its *size*, or *cardinality*, and is signified by the *hash* sign:

```
# {B, NL, L}  = 3
# {GB}        = 1
# GB          illegal, GB is not a set
# Ø           = 0
```

2.11.7 Powersets

The *powerset* of a set S is written

ℙ S

and is the set of all its subsets. For example, the subsets of Benelux are:

```
ℙ {B, NL, L} =
{ Ø,                          the empty set
{B}, {NL}, {L},               all the singletons
{B, NL}, {B, L}, {NL, L},     all the pairs
{B, NL, L}}                   the three elements
```

When a variable is to be declared to have a type that is *set* of elements, the type is the powerset of the type of the elements:

benelux: $\mathbb{P}EU$

This can be read '*benelux* is a *subset* of the set of countries *EU*', or '*benelux* is a set of *EU* countries'.

Note that the size of the powerset of a set is equal to two raised to the power of the size of the set:

$$\# (\mathbb{P}S) \qquad = 2^{\#S} \text{ (for any set S)}$$
$$\# \{B, NL, L\} \qquad = 3$$
$$\# (\mathbb{P} \{B, NL, L\}) \qquad = 8$$

2.11.8 Set inclusion

The operator

$$\subseteq$$

is pronounced 'is included in' or 'is contained in' or 'is a subset of' and tests whether the first set is included in the second set; whether the first is a subset of the second. Every element of the first set is also an element of the second.

In Figure 2.3 the sets *S* and *T* are subsets of some type *X*. *T* is a subset of *S*:

Figure 2.3

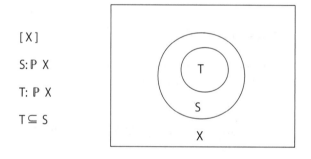

$[X]$

$S: \mathbb{P}\ X$

$T: \mathbb{P}\ X$

$T \subseteq S$

$$\{B, NL\} \subseteq \{B, NL, L\} \qquad \text{this is true}$$
$$\varnothing \subseteq \{B, NL, L\} \qquad \text{this is true}$$
$$\{B, NL, L\} \subseteq \{B, NL, L\} \qquad \text{this is true}$$

The empty set is a *subset* of every set, including itself. But note that the empty set is not a *member* of every set. (The empty set can only be a member of a *set of sets*). An example of an empty set of European Union countries is the set of those countries bordering the Pacific Ocean (that is, none of them).

$$\varnothing \subseteq S \qquad \text{this is true for any set S}$$
$$\varnothing \subseteq \varnothing \qquad \text{empty set is a subset of empty set}$$

Note that testing for the inclusion of a singleton set in another set is the same as testing for that singleton set's element's membership in the set:

$$\{x\} \subseteq S \text{ is the same as } x \in S$$

2.11.9 Union

The *union* of two sets is the set containing all the elements that are in *either* the first set *or* the second set *or* both. The union symbol is sometimes pronounced 'cup'. In Figure 2.4 S and T are both subsets of some type X. The shaded area is the union of S and T:

Figure 2.4

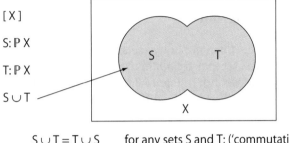

$$S \cup T = T \cup S \quad \text{for any sets S and T; ('commutative')}$$
$$S \cup \emptyset = S \quad \text{for any set S}$$

Examples

$$\{B, D, DK\} \cup \{D, DK, F, I\} = \{B, D, DK, F, I\}$$
$$\{B, D, DK\} \cup \{DK, F, I\} = \{B, D, DK, F, I\}$$
$$\{B, NL, L\} \cup \{GB, IRL\} = \{B, NL, L, GB, IRL\}$$
$$\{B, D, DK\} \cup \emptyset = \{B, D, DK\}$$

2.11.10 Intersection

The *intersection* of two sets is the set containing all the elements that are in both the first set and the second set. The intersection symbol is sometimes pronounced 'cap'. In Figure 2.5 S and T are both subsets of some type X. The area pointed to is the intersection of S and T:

Figure 2.5

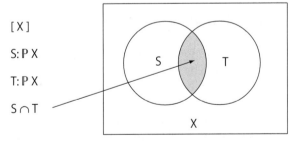

$$S \cap T = T \cap S \quad \text{for any sets S and T; ('commutative')}$$
$$S \cap \emptyset = \emptyset \quad \text{for any set S}$$

Examples

$$\{B, D, DK\} \cap \{D, DK, F, I\} = \{D, DK\}$$
Germany and Denmark are in both sets

{B, D, DK} ∩ {DK, F, I} = {DK}
only Denmark is in both sets. Note {DK}, not just DK

{B, NL, L} ∩ {GB, IRL} = Ø
No country is in both sets

{B, D, DK} ∩ Ø = Ø

2.11.11 Difference

The *difference* of two sets is the set containing all those elements of the first set that are *not* in the second set. It is as if the first set is 'eclipsed' by the second. In Figure 2.6 S and T are both subsets of some type X. The shaded area is the difference of S and T:

Figure 2.6

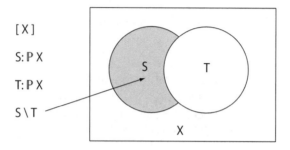

[X]

S: ℙ X

T: ℙ X

S \ T

$S \setminus T \neq T \setminus S$	for any sets S and T (in general not commutative)
$S \setminus Ø = S$	for any set S
$Ø \setminus S = Ø$	for any set S

Example

{B, D, DK, F, I} \ {B, D, GR} = {DK, F, I}
{B, D, DK} \ Ø = {B, D, DK}

2.11.12 Distributed union

The operations described so far have been applied to *two* sets. Sometimes it is useful to be able to refer to the union of several sets; in fact, of a *set* of sets. This can be done with the *distributed union* operator, written as an oversized union operator sign, which applies to a set of sets and results in a set. The distributed union of a set of sets is the set containing just those elements that occur in *at least one of* the component sets.

In Figure 2.7 R, S and T are all subsets of some type X. The shaded area is the distributed union of R, S and T:

Figure 2.7

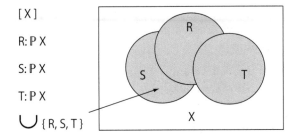

[X]

R: ℙ X

S: ℙ X

T: ℙ X

⋃ { R, S, T }

Example

⋃ { {B, NL, L}, {F, D, L, I}, {GB, GR, B, IRL, DK, E, P} }
= {B, NL, L, F, D, I, GB, GR, IRL, DK, E, P}

2.11.13 Distributed intersection

The *distributed intersection* of a set of sets is the set of elements which are in all of the component sets. The distributed intersection of a set of sets is the set containing just those elements that occur in *all of* the component sets.

In Figure 2.8 *R*, *S* and *T* are all subsets of some type *X*. The small area pointed to is the distributed intersection of *R*, *S* and *T*:

Figure 2.8

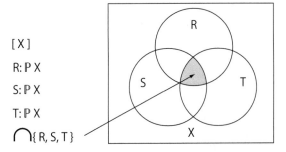

[X]

R: ℙ X

S: ℙ X

T: ℙ X

⋂{ R, S, T }

Example

⋂ { {B, NL, L, GB}, {F, NL, D, L, GB, I}, {GB, GR, IRL, DK, NL, P} }
= {GB, NL}

2.12 Disjoint sets

Sets that are *disjoint* have no elements in common; their intersection is the empty set. This is easily expressed for two sets *S* and *T*

S ∩ T = ∅

For more than two sets it becomes lengthier, since every *pair* of sets must have empty intersections. For example for sets *A*, *B* and *C* to be disjoint:

$A \cap B = \emptyset$ and
$B \cap C = \emptyset$ and
$C \cap A = \emptyset$

In general we can write:

disjoint $\langle S, T \rangle$
disjoint $\langle A, B, C \rangle$

[PERSON]
female, male: $\mathbb{P}$PERSON

disjoint $\langle$female, male$\rangle$

The brackets here are *sequence brackets*. Sequences will be covered in Chapter 12.

2.13   Partition

A *sequence* of sets is said to *partition* another larger set if the sets are disjoint and their distributed union is the entire larger set. For example, the sets *A*, *B* and *C* partition *T* if:

disjoint $\langle A, B, C \rangle$

and

$$\bigcup \{A, B, C\} = T$$

This can be written:

$\langle A, B, C \rangle$ partition T

For example:

$\langle$female, male$\rangle$ partition PERSON

2.14   Summary of notation

$\mathbb{Z}$	the *type* integer (the set of all whole numbers)
$\mathbb{N}$	the *set* of natural numbers ($\{0, 1, 2, \ldots\}$)
$\mathbb{N}_1$	the *set* of *positive* natural numbers ($\{1, 2, \ldots\}$)
$t \in S$	t is an element of S
$t \notin S$	t is not an element of S
$S \subseteq T$	S is contained in T
$\emptyset$ or $\{\}$	the empty set
$\{t_1, t_2, \ldots t_n\}$	the set containing $t_1, t_2, \ldots t_n$

$\mathbb{P}S$	Powerset: the set of all subsets of S
$S \cup T$	Union: elements that are either in S or T or both
$S \cap T$	Intersection: elements that are both in S and in T
$S \setminus T$	Difference: elements that are in S but not in T
#S	Size (cardinality): the number of elements in S
m .. n	the set of integers m to n inclusive
$\bigcup$ SS	the distributed union of the set of sets SS
$\bigcap$ SS	the distributed intersection of the set of sets SS
disjoint sqs	the sets in the sequence sqs are disjoint
sqs partition S	the sets in sqs partition S

EXERCISES

1. Certain people are registered as users of a computer system. At any given time, some of these users are 'logged-in' to the computer. Describe this situation using the concepts of Z covered so far.

2. Extend your description from Question 1 as follows:

   There is a limit (unspecified) to the number of users logged-in at any time.

3. Extend your description from Question 1 as follows:

   All users are either staff users or customer users.

4. Express the following statements using Z notations:

   All the currently logged-in users are staff.

   There are more customer users than staff users.

5. In a modular university course some modules are *acceptable* and others are *compulsory*. Use the names *acceptables* and *compulsories* for the sets of modules. Each student studies modules from two *fields*.

   The acceptable modules for the first field are called *firstAcc* and for the second *secondAcc*:

   firstAcc $\subseteq$ acceptables
   secondAcc $\subseteq$ acceptables

   (a) Write an expression to state that all compulsory modules are also acceptable.
   (b) Write an expression to state that there are three compulsory modules.
   (c) Write an expression to state that the acceptables for the first field are not the same as the acceptables for the second field.
   (d) Write an expression to state that some modules are acceptable for both the first field and the second field.

Using sets to describe a system – a simple example

3.1 Introduction

With only the mathematics covered so far it is possible to describe a very simple system.

This example concerns recording the passengers aboard an aircraft. There are no seat numbers. Passengers are allowed aboard on a first-come-first-served basis. The aircraft has a fixed capacity which must never be exceeded.

The only *basic type* involved here is the set of all possible persons, which we will call *PERSON*.

[PERSON]   the set of all possible uniquely identified persons

Normally, people are identified by name and the possibility of two or more persons having the same name poses difficulties, so we assume that people are identified *uniquely*; for example, by identity-card number or passport number.

The capacity of the aircraft is a natural number which we will call *capacity*. Its actual value is not relevant to the specification; it could even be zero:

capacity: $\mathbb{N}$ the seating capacity of the aircraft

3.2 State-based approach

We describe a system by firstly defining the variables that give its *state* and any invariant properties relating those variables. We also define an operation to set the values of the variables to some suitable *initial state* that satisfies the invariant requirement. We then define *operations* that *change* that state while maintaining the *invariant* properties. We can also define *enquiries* that obtain information about the system without changing its state. Finding the invariant properties that exist between components of a system is a very important early stage of formal specification.

3.3 The state

The state of the aircraft system is given by the set of people on board the aircraft. This can be described by a set of persons, for which we use the variable *onboard*. Its type is a subset of the set *PERSON*:

onboard: $\mathbb{P}$PERSON

The number of persons on board must never exceed the capacity:

#onboard $\leq$ capacity

This is an *invariant* property of the state of the system. No operation will be permitted to lead the system into a state for which it does not hold.

3.4 Initialisation operation

There must be an initial state for the system. The obvious one is where the aircraft is empty. The value of a variable *after* an operation is denoted by its name 'decorated' with a prime sign. For example, the value of the variable *onboard* after an operation is designated by *onboard'* (pronounced 'onboard prime'). The 'undecorated' name (*onboard*) refers to the value *before* the operation.

We will define an initialising operation to states that the new value of the set *onboard* is the empty set:

onboard' $= \emptyset$

The initialised state must satisfy the invariant property. This it clearly does, since the size of the empty set is zero, which is less than or equal to all natural numbers, and so to all possible values of *capacity*.

3.5 Operations

3.5.1 Boarding

There must be an operation to allow a person, *p*, to board the aircraft. This changes the value of *onboard*.

Figure 3.1

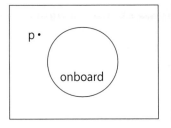

$$onboard' = onboard \cup \{p\}$$

Note that $\{p\}$ is the singleton set containing just the value p. The new value of the variable *onboard* is the same as the union of its old value and the singleton set containing p.

Each normal boarding operation increases the size of the set *onboard* by one, so eventually the size of *onboard* would exceed *capacity*, thus violating the invariant condition. Therefore, it is a necessary *precondition* of this operation that the size of *onboard* before the operation is strictly less than *capacity*:

$$\#onboard < capacity$$

It would clearly be an error to record the boarding of a person who is already recorded as being on board, so a further precondition is:

$$p \notin onboard$$

To summarise:

p: PERSON

p ∉ onboard
#onboard < capacity
onboard' = onboard ∪ {p}

Decisions regarding the behaviour of the system when the preconditions are not satisfied are best deferred. The Z language offers a convenient notation for adding to a specification at a later stage.

3.5.2 Disembark

It is also necessary to have an operation to allow a person to disembark from the aircraft. The effect on *onboard* is:

Figure 3.2

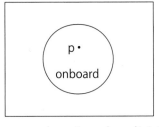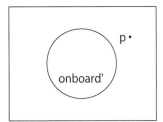

$$onboard' = onboard \setminus \{p\}$$

The new value of the variable *onboard* is the same as the old value of *onboard* with the set containing just *p* removed. The precondition of this operation is that the person *p* must be onboard

$p \in$ onboard

To summarise:

p: PERSON

$p \in$ onboard
onboard' = onboard \ {p}

3.6 Enquiries

3.6.1 Number on board

In addition to operations which change the state of the system it is necessary to have an operation to discover the number of persons on board: *numOnboard*. This has no precondition; it always works. It leaves the value of *onboard* unchanged:

numOnboard: $\mathbb{N}$
numOnboard = #onboard
onboard' = onboard

Note that it is necessary to state *explicitly* that *onboard* does not change. To say nothing about *onboard'* would imply that it could have *any* value after the operation.

3.6.2 Person on board

Finally, a useful enquiry is to discover whether or not a given person, *p*, is on board. The reply will be a value of the free type *RESPONSE*, which we declare:

RESPONSE ::= yes | no

There is no precondition and the state remains unchanged:

p: PERSON
reply: RESPONSE

(($p \in$ onboard and reply = yes)
or
($p \notin$ onboard and reply = no))

onboard' = onboard

The logical operators *and* and *or* will be covered in a later chapter. This section can be read: 'either *p* is onboard and the reply is *yes* or *p* is not onboard and the reply is *no*. The state is unchanged.'

3.7   Conclusion

Although the system described here is very simple, it has been described using the concepts of set theory. The description is not complete since treatment of violation of preconditions has been deferred, but the description will be augmented later. The purpose of this example has been to give a first taste of the use of mathematics to describe a system.

EXERCISES

For a computer system as described in Question 1, Chapter 2:

1.   Discover any invariant properties.
2.   Define a suitable initialisation operation for this system.
3.   Define an operation to register a person as a new user, who is initially not logged-in.
4.   Define an operation to remove a user's registration, when the user is not logged-in.
5.   Define operations for a user to log in and to log out.

CHAPTER 4

Logic

4.1 Introduction

The example at the end of the previous chapter which discovered whether or not a person was on board an aircraft used the *logical operators and* and *or*. This chapter gives a fuller explanation of these and other logical operators.

4.2 Propositional calculus

Propositional calculus is also known as *Boolean algebra* and is named after the mathematician George Boole. It is concerned with statements, called *propositions*, which may be either true or false. The values that the propositions may take are denoted by the words *true* and *false* in Z.

4.3 Operators

Since there are only two possible values that a proposition can take it is practical to explain the action of operators by enumerating all results. This is done using a table called a *truth table*. The following operators can be applied to propositions:

4.3.1 Negation

The *negation* operator is pronounced 'not' and is written:

¬

For any proposition *P*, the truth table for negation is:

P	¬P
false	true
true	false

When *P* is *false*, ¬P is *true*; when *P* is *true*, ¬P is *false*.

4.3.2 Conjunction

The *conjunction* operator is pronounced 'and' and is written:

∧

(To remember this symbol: ∧ looks like the 'A' of 'AND')
Given propositions P and Q, the truth table for conjunction is:

P	Q	$P \wedge Q$
false	false	false
false	true	false
true	false	false
true	true	true

The proposition $P \wedge Q$ is true only when both P is true and Q is true, otherwise it is false.

4.3.3 Disjunction

The *disjunction* operator is pronounced 'or' and is written:

∨

Given propositions P and Q, the truth table for disjunction is:

P	Q	$P \vee Q$
false	false	false
false	true	true
true	false	true
true	true	true

The proposition $P \vee Q$ is true only when either P is true or Q is true or both are true. It is false when both P and Q are false.

4.3.4 Implication

The *implication* operator is pronounced 'implies' and is written:

⇒

The implication

$P \Rightarrow Q$

can be read as: 'if P is true then so is Q'.
Given propositions P and Q, the truth table for implication is:

P	Q	$P \Rightarrow Q$
false	false	true
false	true	true
true	false	false
true	true	true

The proposition $P \Rightarrow Q$ is false only when P is true and Q is false. A useful relationship between implication and disjunction is

$P \Rightarrow Q$ is equivalent to $\neg P \vee Q$

This is useful for removing implications when manipulating expressions.

4.3.5 Equivalence

The *equivalence* operator is pronounced 'is equivalent to' or 'if and only if' and is written:

$$\Leftrightarrow$$

Given propositions P and Q, the truth table for equivalence is:

P	Q	$P \Leftrightarrow Q$
false	false	true
false	true	false
true	false	false
true	true	true

The proposition $P \Leftrightarrow Q$ is true if P always has the same truth value as Q. The equivalence given above for implication can be written:

$$P \Rightarrow Q \Leftrightarrow \neg P \vee Q$$

A useful law relating implication to equivalence is:

$$(P \Rightarrow Q) \wedge (Q \Rightarrow P) \Leftrightarrow (P \Leftrightarrow Q)$$

4.4 De Morgan's laws

The following important laws relating negation, conjunction and disjunction are due to the mathematician Augustus de Morgan:

$$\neg(P \wedge Q) \Leftrightarrow \neg P \vee \neg Q$$
$$\neg(P \vee Q) \Leftrightarrow \neg P \wedge \neg Q$$

These are useful for simplifying expressions.

4.5 Demonstrating laws

A *law* is a relationship which holds good irrespective of the actual values of the propositions involved. Truth tables can be used to demonstrate the validity of a law. For example, to show the validity of the first of de Morgan's laws given above:

$$\neg(P \wedge Q) \Leftrightarrow \neg P \vee \neg Q$$

we complete the truth table, building towards the expression to be compared:

P	Q	$P \wedge Q$	$\neg (P \wedge Q)$
false	false	false	true
false	true	false	true
true	false	false	true
true	true	true	false

$\neg P$	$\neg Q$	$\neg P \vee \neg Q$	$\neg (P \wedge Q) \Leftrightarrow \neg P \vee \neg Q$
true	true	true	true
true	false	true	true
false	true	true	true
false	false	false	true

4.6 Using laws

Laws are used to prove that two statements in the propositional calculus, which are not necessarily identical, are equivalent. In formal specification laws are used in chains of transformations called *proofs* which can verify that a specification is consistent and make deductions about the behaviour of a system from its specification.

4.7 Example proof – exclusive-or

The *exclusive-or* operator (often written *xor*) is sometimes needed to relate two propositions. It gives true if one or other proposition is true but not both. (The disjunction operator is an *inclusive* or.) It is not a basic operator of propositional calculus but it can be formulated from the existing operators in (at least) two ways:

$$P \text{ xor } Q \Leftrightarrow (P \vee Q) \wedge \neg (P \wedge Q)$$
$$P \text{ xor } Q \Leftrightarrow (P \wedge \neg Q) \vee (\neg P \wedge Q)$$

These could be shown to be equivalent by means of a truth table, but a proof by application of laws taken from the list which follows is also possible and such a proof is more practical in cases where more than two propositions are involved.

The proof which follows is deliberately made very laborious so that every transformation will be visible and justified. In practice, many simple transformations are made from one line to the next and simple laws such as commutativity are not cited.

In general, deriving proofs is a mathematical skill which must be learned and which is beyond the scope of this book. Software tools are now available to assist in the derivation of proofs.

$$(P \vee Q) \wedge \neg (P \wedge Q) \qquad \text{first formulation}$$

$$\Leftrightarrow$$

$$(P \vee Q) \wedge (\neg P \vee \neg Q) \qquad \text{by de Morgan's } and$$

$\Leftrightarrow$

$((P \lor Q) \land \neg P)$
$\lor ((P \lor Q) \land \neg Q)$ by distribution of *or* over *and*

$\Leftrightarrow$

$(\neg P \land (P \lor Q))$
$\lor (\neg Q \land (P \lor Q))$ by commutativity of *and* (twice)

$\Leftrightarrow$

$((\neg P \land P) \lor (\neg P \land Q))$
$\lor ((\neg Q \land P) \lor (\neg Q \land Q))$ by distribution of *or* over *and*

$\Leftrightarrow$

$((P \land \neg P) \lor (\neg P \land Q))$
$\lor ((\neg Q \land P) \lor (Q \land \neg Q))$ commutative *and* (twice)

$\Leftrightarrow$

$(\text{false} \lor (\neg P \land Q))$
$\lor ((\neg Q \land P) \lor \text{false})$ by contradiction (twice)

$\Leftrightarrow$

$((\neg P \land Q) \lor \text{false})$
$\lor ((\neg Q \land P) \lor \text{false})$ by commutativity of *or*

$\Leftrightarrow$

$(\neg P \land Q)$
$\lor (\neg Q \land P)$ by *or* simplification 3 (twice)

$\Leftrightarrow$

$(\neg P \land Q)$
$\lor (P \land \neg Q)$ by commutativity of *and*

$\Leftrightarrow$

$(P \land \neg Q) \lor (\neg P \land Q)$ by commutativity of *or*

4.8   Laws about logical operators

Given propositions *P*, *Q* and *R*:

Law	Name
$(P \land Q) \Leftrightarrow (Q \land P)$	commutativity of *and*
$(P \lor Q) \Leftrightarrow (Q \lor P)$	commutativity of *or*
$(P \Leftrightarrow Q) \Leftrightarrow (Q \Leftrightarrow P)$	commutativity of *equivalence*
$P \land (Q \land R) \Leftrightarrow (P \land Q) \land R$	
$\Leftrightarrow P \land Q \land R$	associativity of *and*
$P \lor (Q \lor R) \Leftrightarrow (P \lor Q) \lor R$	
$\Leftrightarrow P \lor Q \lor R$	associativity of *or*
$P \land (Q \lor R) \Leftrightarrow (P \land Q) \lor (P \land R)$	distribution of *or* over *and*
$P \lor (Q \land R) \Leftrightarrow (P \lor Q) \land (P \lor R)$	distribution of *and* over *or*
$\neg(P \land Q) \Leftrightarrow \neg P \lor \neg Q$	de Morgan's *and*

$$\neg(P \lor Q) \Leftrightarrow \neg P \land \neg Q \qquad \text{de Morgan's } or$$
$$\neg(\neg P) \Leftrightarrow P \qquad \text{negation}$$
$$P \lor \neg P \Leftrightarrow \text{true} \qquad \text{excluded middle}$$
$$P \land \neg P \Leftrightarrow \text{false} \qquad \text{contradiction}$$
$$P \Rightarrow Q \Leftrightarrow \neg P \lor Q \qquad \text{implication}$$
$$(P \Leftrightarrow Q) \Leftrightarrow (P \Rightarrow Q) \land (Q \Rightarrow P) \qquad \text{equality}$$
$$P \lor P \Leftrightarrow P \qquad or \text{ simplification 1}$$
$$P \lor \text{true} \Leftrightarrow \text{true} \qquad or \text{ simplification 2}$$
$$P \lor \text{false} \Leftrightarrow P \qquad or \text{ simplification 3}$$
$$P \lor (P \land Q) \Leftrightarrow P \qquad or \text{ simplification 4}$$
$$P \land P \Leftrightarrow P \qquad and \text{ simplification 1}$$
$$P \land \text{true} \Leftrightarrow P \qquad and \text{ simplification 2}$$
$$P \land \text{false} \Leftrightarrow \text{false} \qquad and \text{ simplification 3}$$
$$P \land (P \lor Q) \Leftrightarrow P \qquad and \text{ simplification 4}$$

Precedence (highest to lowest)

$$\neg$$
$$\land$$
$$\lor$$
$$\Rightarrow$$
$$\Leftrightarrow$$

4.9 Summary of notation

true, false	logical constants
$\neg P$	negation: 'not P'
$P \land Q$	conjunction: 'P and Q'
$P \lor Q$	disjunction: 'P or Q'
$P \Rightarrow Q$	implication: 'P implies Q' or 'if P then Q'
$P \Leftrightarrow Q$	equivalence: 'P is logically equivalent to Q'
$t_1 = t_2$	equality between terms
$t_1 \neq t_2$	$\neg(t_1 = t_2)$

EXERCISES

1. Show by truth table that:

    $$(P \Rightarrow Q) \Leftrightarrow (\neg P \lor Q)$$

2. Show by truth table that:

    $$((P \Rightarrow Q) \land (Q \Rightarrow P)) \Leftrightarrow (P \Leftrightarrow Q)$$

3. By using laws from this chapter simplify:

    $$\neg(p \notin \text{onboard} \land \#\text{onboard} < \text{capacity})$$

4. By using laws from this chapter simplify:

   $(a \wedge b) \vee (a \wedge c) \vee (a \wedge \neg c)$

5. Given

   $p \in loggedIn \Rightarrow p \in user$

   convince yourself that

   $p \in loggedIn \wedge p \in user$

   can be simplified to

   $p \in loggedIn$

6. Use de Morgan's laws to simplify the following expression:

   $x \neq 2 \vee x \neq 6$

7. Simplify the following expression:

   $s = t \wedge s \neq EOF \wedge t \neq EOF$

8. Simplify the following expression:

   $x = x \wedge (x \leq y \vee x = y)$

9. Simplify the following expression:

   $x = 0 \wedge x \geq 0$

10. Simplify the following expression:

    $\neg(age \geq 16 \vee student)$

The example extended

5.1 Full definition of boarding operation

The definitions of the operations for boarding and disembarking from the aircraft in the example of Chapter 3 did not consider what was to happen if the precondition of an operation was not fulfilled. Now this will be rectified. Each operation will have an additional variable, *reply*, which gives a response to indicate what happened during the operation. The response will be a value of the type *RESPONSE*:

RESPONSE ::= OK | twoErrors | onBoard | full | notOnBoard

5.1.1 Board

The operation to board the aircraft can now be given. Either:

▶ *p* is not on board and the aircraft full and *p* gets included in *onboard* and reply is *OK*;

▶ or *p* is already on board and the aircraft is full and the set *onboard* is unchanged and reply is *twoErrors*;

▶ or *p* is already on board and the aircraft is not full and the set *onboard* is unchanged and reply is *onBoard*;

▶ or p is not on board and the aircraft is full and the set *onboard* is unchanged and reply is *full*.

p: PERSON
reply: RESPONSE

$(p \notin onboard \land \#onboard < capacity \land$
$onboard' = onboard \cup \{p\} \land reply = OK)$

$\lor$

$(p \in onboard \land \#onboard = capacity \land$
$onboard' = onboard \land reply = twoErrors)$

$\lor$

$(p \in onboard \land \#onboard < capacity \land$
$onboard' = onboard \land reply = onBoard)$

$\lor$

$(p \notin onboard \land \#onboard = capacity \land$
$onboard' = onboard \land reply = full)$

5.1.2   Disembark

The operation to disembark from the aircraft can now be given. Either:

▸ *p* is on board and *p* gets removed from *onboard* and reply is *OK*;

▸ or *p* is not on board and the set *onboard* is unchanged and reply is *notOnBoard*.

p: PERSON
reply: RESPONSE

(p ∈ onboard ∧
onboard' = onboard \ {p} ∧ reply = OK)

∨

(p ∉ onboard ∧
onboard' = onboard ∧ reply = notOnBoard)

5.2   A better way

As can be seen, this way of defining the operations in full begins to get complicated. A much better, *modular*, approach using *schemas* will be introduced in the next chapter.

EXERCISES

Referring to Question 1, Chapter 2, and its development in exercises of Chapter 3, give full descriptions in the manner of this chapter for:

1. A suitable type for the response from any of the following operations.
2. The operation to register a new user.
3. The operation to remove a user's registration.
4. The operation to log in.
5. The operation to log out.

Schemas

6.1 Schemas

A specification document in Z consists of narrative text written in a natural language such as English, interspersed with formal descriptions written in the Z notation. As a way of making a clear separation between these two components a graphical format called the *schema* (plural *schemas*) was devised. The schema also has various useful mathematical properties.

Here is an example of a schema:

$$\begin{array}{|l}\hline S \\\hline a, b: \qquad \mathbb{N} \\\hline a < b \\\hline\end{array}$$

The schema is referred to by the name S and it declares two *variables*, a and b. It also contains a *constraining predicate* which states that a must be less than b.

A schema can also be written in an equivalent *linear* form, which is more convenient for small schemas:

$$S == [\, a, b: \mathbb{N} \mid a < b \,]$$

The operator

$$==$$

means 'stands for'.

The general form of a schema is:

$$\begin{array}{|l}\hline SchemaName \\\hline Declarations \\\hline Predicate \\\hline\end{array}$$

and the form of the linear schema is

$$SchemaName == [\, declarations \mid predicate \,]$$

It is possible to have an *anonymous* schema, in which case the schema name would be omitted. Furthermore, it is possible to have a schema with no predicate part. In this case the schema would simply declare a new variable or variables without applying a constraining predicate.

A variable introduced by a schema is *local* to that schema and may only be referenced in another schema by explicitly *including* the variable's defining schema. This is sometimes inconvenient and it is also possible to introduce variables which are available throughout the specification. These are known as *global* variables and are introduced by an *axiomatic* definition. Such values cannot be changed by operations of the specification.

For example, the fixed capacity of an aircraft is introduced as a global variable by:

$$\mathrm{capacity:} \qquad \mathbb{N}$$

If you wish to add a constraining predicate to the variable you can use the general form:

$$\begin{array}{|l}
\textit{Declarations} \\
\hline
\textit{Predicate}
\end{array}$$

For example, to introduce a limit to the number of participants who may enrol on a course, *maxOnCourse*, where this limit must be in the range 6 to 30, you could use the following:

$$\begin{array}{|l}
\mathrm{maxOnCourse:} \\
\hline
\mathrm{maxOnCourse} \in 6 \mathinner{\ldotp\ldotp} 30
\end{array}$$

Schemas can make reference to *capacity* and *maxOnCourse* without explicitly including their defining schemas:

$$\begin{array}{|l|}
\hline
\text{Course} \\
\hline
\mathrm{numberEnrolled:}\ \mathbb{N} \\
\hline
\mathrm{numberEnrolled} \leq \mathrm{maxOnCourse} \\
\hline
\end{array}$$

If a schema contains several lines of declarations then each line is regarded as being terminated by a semicolon. Furthermore, if the predicate part consists of more than one line then the lines are regarded as being joined by *and* operators. For example:

```
__Class_____
  lecturer:      PERSON
  students:      ℙPERSON
 _____
  lecturer ∉ students
  #students ≤ maxOnCourse
 _____
```

is an abbreviation of

```
__Class_____
  lecturer:      PERSON    ;
  students:      ℙPERSON   ;
 _____
  lecturer ∉ students        ∧
  #students ≤ maxOnCourse
 _____
```

6.2 Schema calculus

Schemas can be regarded as units and manipulated by various operators that are analogous to the logical operators.

6.2.1 Decoration

The schema name S decorated with a prime, S', is defined to be the same as the schema S with all its *variables* decorated with a prime. It is used to signify the value of a schema *after* some operation has been carried out. It is as if the schema S' had been defined:

```
__S'_____
  a', b':         ℕ
 _____
  a' < b'
 _____
```

6.2.2 Inclusion

The name of a schema can be included in the declarations of another schema. The effect is for the included schema to be *textually imported*: its declarations are merged with those of the including schema and its predicate part is conjoined ('*anded*') with that of the including schema. (It follows that any variables that have the same name in each schema must be of the same type. If not then the schema conjunction is illegal.)

$$
\begin{array}{|l}
\_\text{IncludeS}_____ \\
\quad c: \qquad\qquad \mathbb{N} \\
\quad S \\
\hline
\quad c < 10 \\
\end{array}
$$

means

$$
\begin{array}{|l}
\_\text{IncludeS}_____ \\
\quad c: \qquad\qquad \mathbb{N} \\
\quad a, b: \qquad\quad\ \mathbb{N} \\
\hline
\quad c < 10 \\
\quad a < b \\
\end{array}
$$

6.2.3 Schema conjunction

Two schemas can be joined by a *schema conjunction* operator, written like the *logical* conjunction operator. The effect is to make a new schema with the declarations of the two component schemas merged and their predicates conjoined ('*anded*'). Given S as before and T:

$$
\begin{array}{|l}
\_T_____ \\
\quad b, c: \qquad\qquad \mathbb{N} \\
\hline
\quad b < c \\
\end{array}
$$

$$\text{SandT} == S \wedge T$$

means

$$
\begin{array}{|l}
\_\text{SandT}_____ \\
\quad a, b, c: \qquad\qquad \mathbb{N} \\
\hline
\quad a < b \\
\quad b < c \\
\end{array}
$$

Variables with the same name, such as the two b's here, are merged if they have the same type. If not then the schema conjunction is illegal.

6.2.4 Schema disjunction

Two schemas can be joined by a *schema disjunction* operator, written just like the logical disjunction. The effect is to make a new schema with the

declarations of the two component schemas merged and their predicates
disjoined ('ored'). (It follows that any variables that have the same name
in each schema must be of the same type. If not then the schema
conjunction is illegal.) Given S and T as before:

$$SorT == S \lor T$$

means

```
___SorT_____
|
| a, b, c:        ℕ
|_____
|
| a < b ∨ b < c
|_____
```

6.2.5 Delta convention

The convention that the value of a variable before an operation is denoted
by the undecorated name of the variable, and the value after an operation
by the name decorated by a prime (') character, is used in the *delta*
naming convention. By convention, a schema with the Greek character
capital delta ('Δ') as the first character of its name, such as ΔS, is defined
to be:

```
___ΔS_____
|
| a, b            ℕ
| a', b':         ℕ
|_____
|
| a < b
| a' < b'
|_____
```

The Greek delta character, in ΔS, is used, as in other areas of
mathematics, to signify a change in S.

6.2.6 Xi convention

By convention, a schema with the Greek character capital *xi* (Ξ) as the
first character of its name, such as ΞS, is defined to be the same as ΔS but
with the constraint that the new value of every variable is the same as the
old. This Greek symbol is chosen for its visual similarity to the *equivalence*
symbol, $\equiv$, showing that the new state is equivalent to the old. It is as if the
schema ΞS were written:

$$
\begin{array}{|l}
\hline
\underline{\Xi S} \\
\quad a, b \qquad\qquad \mathbb{N} \\
\quad a', b': \qquad\quad \mathbb{N} \\
\hline
\quad a < b \\
\quad a' < b' \\
\quad a = a' \\
\quad b = b' \\
\hline
\end{array}
$$

6.3 Decoration of input and output variables

A convention is used to decorate the variables of a schema which specifies an operation. Finishing the variable's name with a question mark (?) indicates that the variable is an *input* to the schema. Finishing the variable's name with an exclamation mark (!) indicates that the variable is an *output* from the schema. Note that the question mark and exclamation mark are simply characters in the variable's name.

6.4 Simple example of schema with input and output

$$
\begin{array}{|l}
\hline
\underline{Add} \\
\quad a?, b?: \qquad\quad \mathbb{N} \\
\quad sum!: \qquad\qquad \mathbb{N} \\
\hline
\quad sum! = a? + b? \\
\hline
\end{array}
$$

6.5 Example of schemas with input

The display of a computer terminal shows lines of characters with each line consisting of a fixed number of columns containing a character in a fixed-width typeface. A *cursor* marks a current position of interest on the display. The user can press cursor-control *keys* on the keyboard, some of which directly control the position of the cursor.

$$KEY ::= home \mid return \mid left \mid right \mid up \mid down$$

$$
\begin{array}{|l}
\hline
\quad numLines: \qquad\quad \mathbb{N} \\
\quad numColumns: \qquad \mathbb{N} \\
\hline
\quad 1 \leq numLines \\
\quad 1 \leq numColumns \\
\hline
\end{array}
$$

The lines are numbered from 1 to *numLines* down the display and the columns are numbered 1 to *numColumns* across the display. (A display with fewer than on lines, or fewer than one column is useless.)

Figure 6.1

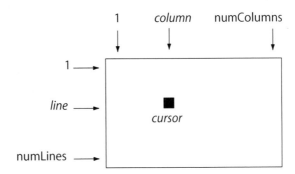

6.5.1 The state

At any time the cursor is within the bounds of the display. The state of the cursor can be described by the schema *Cursor:*

┌─ Cursor ─────────────────────
│ line: $\mathbb{N}$
│ column: $\mathbb{N}$
├──────────────────────────────
│ line $\in$ 1 .. numLines
│ column $\in$ 1 .. numColumns
└──────────────────────────────

6.5.2 Home key

The operations for moving the cursor can be built up one at a time. The simplest is the response to the *home* key. It causes the cursor to move to the top-left corner of the display.

┌─ HomeKey ─────────────────────
│ ΔCursor
│ key?:   KEY
├──────────────────────────────
│ key? = home
│ line' = 1
│ column' = 1
└──────────────────────────────

Reminder: We do not need to declare the schema Δ*Cursor* since it is automatically defined to be:

```
┌─ ΔCursor ──────────────────────
│ line, line':        ℕ
│ column, column':  ℕ
├────────────────────────────────
│ line ∈ 1 .. numLines
│ line' ∈ 1 .. numLines
│ column ∈ 1 .. numColumns
│ column' ∈ 1 .. numColumns
└────────────────────────────────
```

6.5.3   Down key

The action for responding to the *down* key is given next. It causes the cursor to move to the same column position on the next line down. It is easiest to start by dealing with what happens if the cursor is *not* on the bottom line of the display.

```
┌─ DownKeyNormal ────────────
│ ΔCursor
│ key?:            KEY
├────────────────────────────
│ key? = down
│ line < numLines
│ line' = line + 1
│ column' = column
└────────────────────────────
```

The next schema deals with what happens when the cursor *is* on the bottom line of the display.

```
┌─ DownKeyAtBottom ──────────
│ ΔCursor
│ key?:            KEY
├────────────────────────────
│ key? = down
│ line = numLines
│ line' = 1
│ column' = column
└────────────────────────────
```

Note that the cursor has been defined to *wrap round* to the top line of the display.

The full behaviour is given by:

DownKey == DownKeyNormal ∨ DownKeyAtBottom

The behaviour of the down key is defined by 'oring' the 'normal' behaviour of the down key with the behaviour of the down key when at the bottom.

6.5.4　Return key

The response to the *return* key is to move to the leftmost column of the next line down or the top line if the cursor was on the bottom line. For contrast this is given as a single schema:

```
┌─ ReturnKey ─────────────────────────
│ ΔCursor
│ key?:          KEY
├─────────────────────────────────────
│ key? = return
│ column' = 1
│ ((line < numLines ∧ line' = line + 1)
│  ∨
│  (line = numLines ∧ line' = 1))
└─────────────────────────────────────
```

6.5.5　Right key

Next, the operation for moving right is given. It is easiest to deal first with what happens when the cursor is *not* at the far right of the display:

```
┌─ RightKeyNormal ─────────────
│ ΔCursor
│ key?:          KEY
├──────────────────────────────
│ key? = right
│ column < numColumns
│ column' = column + 1
│ line' = line
└──────────────────────────────
```

The next schema deals with the situation when the cursor *is* at the end of a line (other than the *bottom* line of the display). Note that the cursor wraps round to the start of the next line:

```
┌─ RightKeyAtEnd ──────────────
│ ΔCursor
│ key?:          KEY
├──────────────────────────────
│ key? = right
│ column = numColumns
│ column' = 1
│ line < numLines
│ line' = line + 1
└──────────────────────────────
```

Finally, a separate schema deals with the situation where the cursor *is* at the end of the *bottom* line. The cursor wraps round to the left of the top line:

```
  ┌─ RightKeyAtBottom ──────────
  │ ΔCursor
  │ key?:              KEY
  ├─────────────────────────
  │ key? = right
  │ column = numColumns
  │ column' = 1
  │ line = numLines
  │ line' = 1
  └─────────────────────────
```

These schemas can be combined to form one schema that defines the response of the cursor to the right key in all initial positions of the cursor:

RightKey ==
RightKeyNormal ∨ RightKeyAtEnd ∨ RightKeyAtBottom

For the sake of illustration here is the expansion of *RightKey*:

```
  ┌─ RightKey ──────────────────
  │ ΔCursor
  │ key?:              KEY
  ├─────────────────────────
  │ (key? = right ∧
  │ column < numColumns ∧
  │ column' = column + 1 ∧
  │ line' = line)
  │
  │ ∨
  │ (key? = right ∧
  │ column = numColumns ∧
  │ column' = 1 ∧
  │ line < numLines ∧
  │ line' = line + 1)
  │
  │ ∨
  │ (key? = right ∧
  │ column = numColumns ∧
  │ column' = 1 ∧
  │ line = numLines ∧
  │ line' = 1)
  └─────────────────────────
```

RightKey can be simplified to

```
┌─ RightKey ──────────────────────┐
│ ΔCursor                          │
│ key?:            KEY             │
├──────────────────────────────────│
│ key? = right ∧                   │
│ ((column < numColumns ∧          │
│   column' = column + 1 ∧         │
│   line' = line)                  │
│ ∨                                │
│   (column = numColumns ∧         │
│   column' = 1 ∧                  │
│     (line < numLines ∧           │
│     line' = line + 1)            │
│ ∨                                │
│   (line = numLines ∧             │
│   line' = 1)))                   │
└──────────────────────────────────┘
```

Of course, the behaviour of the cursor at the end of the line and at the bottom-right of the display need not be defined as here. The style used here of defining separate schemas to describe the behaviour in these situations makes it easier to understand what happens in these cases.

6.5.6 Cursor-control key action

The action of the cursor on the pressing of any of these *cursor-control* keys can be defined by

CursorControlKey ==
HomeKey ∨ ReturnKey ∨ UpKey ∨ DownKey ∨ LeftKey ∨ RightKey

6.6 Further operations on schemas

6.6.1 Renaming

The observations in a schema may be *renamed* by the following form:

schemaName [newName / oldName]

For example, given:

```
┌─ Aircraft ──────────────────┐
│ onboard:      ℙPERSON         │
├──────────────────────────────│
│ #onboard ≤ capacity          │
└──────────────────────────────┘
```

then

$$Ship == Aircraft\ [passengers\ /\ onboard]$$

gives:

```
┌─ Ship ──────────────────────
│
│  passengers:    PPERSON
│ ────────────────────────────
│  #passengers ≤ capacity
│
└─────────────────────────────
```

6.6.2 Hiding

The schema *hiding* operator hides specified variables so that they are no longer variables of the schema and simply become local variables of existential operators in the predicate part of the schema. For example, given:

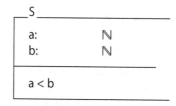

then

$$BHidden == S \setminus (b)$$

gives the schema:

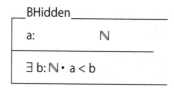

Several variable names can be given in the brackets.

6.6.3 Projection

Schema *projection* is similar to hiding except *all but* the named variables are hidden. Given S as above then

$$AProjected == S \upharpoonright (a)$$

gives the schema:

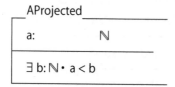

6.6.4 Schema composition

The *composition* of schema *S* with schema *T* is written:

S ⨾ T

and signifies the effect of doing *S*, then doing *T*. It is equivalent to renaming the variables describing the after state of *S* to some temporary names and the equivalent variables describing the before state of *T* with the same temporary names and then hiding the temporary names.

For example, to show the effect of pressing the right-key and then the left-key on a visual display, using the definition of *CursorControlKey*:

PressRight == CursorControlKey ∧ [key?: KEY | key? = right]
PressLeft == CursorControlKey ∧ [key?: KEY | key? = left]

PressRight ⨾ PressLeft

==

PressRight [tempCol / column', tempLine / line'] ∧
PressLeft [tempCol / column, tempLine / line]
\ (tempCol, tempLine)

6.7 Overall structure of a Z specification document

A Z specification document consists of mathematical text in the Z notation, interleaved with explanatory text in a natural language. The explanatory text should be expressed in terms of the problem and should not refer directly to the mathematical formulation. This rule is broken only in the case of documents intended as tutorials on Z.

6.7.1 Sections of a Z document

The sections of a Z document are as follows:

▶ Introduction.
▶ The types used in the specification (their introduction is sometimes deferred until they are needed).
▶ The state and its invariant properties.
▶ An operation to set the variables to some initial state.
▶ Operations and enquiries.
▶ Error handling.
▶ Final versions of operations and enquiries.

Some simple examples of Z specification documents appear in the next chapter.

6.8 Summary of notation

```
┌─ SchemaName ──────────────
│ declarations
├──────────────────────────
│ predicate
└──────────────────────────
```

SchemaName == [declarations | predicate]

6.8.1 Axiomatic definition

```
│ declarations
├──────────────────────────
│ predicate
```

6.8.2 Decoration

```
┌─ S ───────────────────────
│ a, b:            ℕ
├──────────────────────────
│ a < b
└──────────────────────────
```

SPrime == S'

```
┌─ SPrime ──────────────────
│ a', b':          ℕ
├──────────────────────────
│ a' < b'
└──────────────────────────
```

6.8.3 Delta convention

```
┌─ ΔS ──────────────────────
│ a, b            ℕ
│ a', b':         ℕ
├──────────────────────────
│ a < b
│ a' < b'
└──────────────────────────
```

6.8.4 Xi convention

```
┌─ΞS─────────────────────
│  a, b          ℕ
│  a', b':       ℕ
├─────────────────────────
│  a < b
│  a' < b'
│  a = a'
│  b = b'
└─────────────────────────
```

6.8.5 Inclusion

```
┌─IncludeS────────────────
│  c:            ℕ
│  S
├─────────────────────────
│  c < 10
└─────────────────────────
```

==

```
┌─IncludeS────────────────
│  c:            ℕ
│  a, b:         ℕ
├─────────────────────────
│  c < 10
│  a < b
└─────────────────────────
```

6.8.6 Conjunction

```
┌─T───────────────────────
│  b, c:         ℕ
├─────────────────────────
│  b < c
└─────────────────────────
```

SandT == S ∧ T
==

```
┌─SandT───────────────────
│  a, b, c:      ℕ
├─────────────────────────
│  a < b
│  b < c
└─────────────────────────
```

6.8.7 Disjunction

SorT == S ∨ T
==

```
__SorT______________________
| a, b, c:        ℕ
|____________________________
| a < b ∨ b < c
|____________________________
```

S[new / old,...]	schema renaming
$S \setminus (x_1, x_2, \ldots, x_n)$	schema hiding
$S \upharpoonright (x_1, x_2, \ldots, x_n)$	schema projection
pre S	precondition of S
$S \fatsemi T$	schema composition: S, then T

EXERCISES

1. Define a schema *LinesRemaining* which delivers the number of lines below the cursor as an output parameter.

   Make use of schemas from the examples in this chapter.
2. Define a schema *UpKey* to define the operation of pressing the *up* key.
3. Define a schema *LeftKey* to define the operation of pressing the *left* key.
4. Devise a schema to define pressing the *down* key where the cursor does not move at all if it is already on the bottom line of the screen.

   Make use of schemas from the examples in this chapter and from your solutions to the previous exercises.
5. Devise a schema to define pressing the *right* key where the cursor does not move at all if it is already on the last column of the screen.

   Make use of schemas from the examples in this chapter and from your solutions to the previous exercises.
6. The Houses of Parliament (*HP*) consist of Members of Parliament (*MPs*), some of whom are in the *Cabinet*. There is an MP called the Prime Minister (*PM*) who is in the Cabinet.

   The only type involved is:

   [PERSON] the set of all persons

   The *state* of the Houses of Parliament is described by the schema *HP*:

```
┌─ HP ──────────────────────
│
│  MPs:          ℙPERSON
│  Cabinet:      ℙPERSON
│  PM:           PERSON
│ ─────────────────────────
│  Cabinet ⊆ MPs
│  PM ∈ Cabinet
└───────────────────────────
```

(a) Does the specification state that the Prime Minister has to be a Member of Parliament? If so, how?

(b) What would you add to the schema *HP* to have a Deputy Prime Minister (*DPM*), who is also in the Cabinet?

(c) An operation *ReplacePM* replaces the Prime Minister with a person *newPM?*.

```
┌─ ReplacePM ───────────────────
│
│  ΔHP
│  newPM?: PERSON
│ ─────────────────────────────
│  newPM? ∈ MPs
│  newPM? ≠ PM
│  Cabinet = Cabinet ∪ {newPM?}
│  PM' = newPM?
│  MPs' = MPs
└───────────────────────────────
```

Why does the schema include the line:

$$newPM? \neq PM$$

(d) Does the new Prime Minister have to be chosen from the Cabinet?

(e) Does the outgoing Prime Minister have to leave the Cabinet?

(f) May the outgoing Prime Minister leave the Cabinet?

7. Two operations, *ChangeCabinet1* and *ChangeCabinet2,* are proposed:

```
┌─ ChangeCabinet1 ──────────
│
│  ΔHP
│  newCab?: ℙPERSON
│ ─────────────────────────
│  newCab? ⊆ MPs
│  Cabinet' = newCab?
│  PM' = PM
│  MPs' = MPs
└───────────────────────────
```

ChangeCabinet2
_____

ΔHP
newCab?: $\mathbb{P}$PERSON

_____

newCab? $\subseteq$ MPs
newCab? $\cap$ Cabinet $= \varnothing$
Cabinet' = newCab?
PM' = PM
MPs' = MPs

(a) Explain why the line:

$$newCab? \subseteq MPs$$

is included.

(b) Explain the difference between the effect of *ChangeCabinet1* and *ChangeCabinet2*.

(c) Explain the logical error in *ChangeCabinet2*.

Examples of Z specification documents

7.1 Introduction

We now re-express the aircraft example of Chapter 3 as a Z specification using schemas. This specification concerns recording the passengers aboard an aircraft. There are no seat numbers; passengers are allowed aboard on a first-come-first-served basis.

7.2 The types

The only *basic type* involved here is the set of all possible persons, *PERSON*:

> [PERSON]   the set of all possible uniquely identified persons

The aircraft has a fixed capacity:

> | capacity: $\mathbb{N}$

7.3 The state

The state of the system is given by the set of persons on board the aircraft. The number of persons on board must never exceed the capacity. This is the state's *invariant* property.

$$
\begin{array}{|l}
\hline
\_Aircraft _____ \\
onboard: \qquad \mathbb{P}PERSON \\
\hline
\#onboard \leq capacity \\
\hline
\end{array}
$$

The state before and after an operation is described by the schema $\Delta Aircraft$, which has its conventional meaning:

```
┌─ΔAircraft ──────────────────┐
│ onboard:          ℙPERSON    │
│ onboard':         ℙPERSON    │
├─────────────────────────────┤
│ #onboard ≤ capacity          │
│ #onboard' ≤ capacity         │
└─────────────────────────────┘
```

7.4 Initialisation operation

There must be an initial state for the system. The obvious one is where the aircraft is empty. A suitable initialisation operation sets a new value to the variable:

```
┌─Init ────────────────┐
│ Aircraft'            │
├──────────────────────┤
│ onboard' = ∅         │
└──────────────────────┘
```

The initialised state must satisfy the state's invariant property. This it clearly does, since the size of the empty set is zero, which is less than or equal to all natural numbers and so to all possible values of *capacity*.

7.5 Operations

7.5.1 Boarding

There must be an operation to allow a person $p?$ to board the aircraft. A first version of this is called $Board_0$:

```
┌─Board₀ ──────────────────────┐
│ ΔAircraft                    │
│ p?:          PERSON          │
├──────────────────────────────┤
│ p? ∉ onboard                 │
│ #onboard < capacity          │
│ onboard' = onboard ∪ {p?}    │
└──────────────────────────────┘
```

7.5.2 Disembarking

It is also necessary to have an operation to allow a person $p?$ to disembark from the aircraft. A first version of this is $Disembark_0$:

```
__Disembark₀_____
 ΔAircraft
 p?:        PERSON
_____
 p? ∈ onboard
 onboard' = onboard \ {p?}
_____
```

7.6   Enquiry operations

These operations leave the state unchanged and therefore use the schema:

ΞAircraft

which has its (automatic) conventional meaning:

```
__ΞAircraft_____
 onboard:          ℙPERSON
 onboard':         ℙPERSON
_____
 #onboard ≤ capacity
 #onboard' ≤ capacity
 onboard = onboard'
_____
```

7.6.1   Number on board

In addition to operations which change the state of the system it is necessary to have an operation to discover the number of persons on board:

```
__Number_____
 ΞAircraft
 numOnboard!:    ℕ
_____
 numOnboard! = #onboard
_____
```

7.6.2   Person on board

Furthermore, a useful enquiry is to discover whether or not a given person p? is on board. The data type *YESORNO* is defined to provide suitable values for the reply and is used in the schema *OnBoard*:

YESORNO ::= yes | no

```
┌─ OnBoard ─────────────────────
│ ΞAircraft
│ p?:        PERSON
│ reply!:    YESORNO
├───────────────────────────────
│ (p? ∈ onboard ∧ reply! = yes)
│ ∨
│ (p? ∉ onboard ∧ reply! = no)
└───────────────────────────────
```

7.7   Dealing with errors

The schemas $Board_0$ and $Disembark_0$ do not state what happens if their preconditions are not satisfied. The schema calculus of Z allows these schemas to be extended. First we define a small schema $OKMessage$ to give the reply OK in the event of success:

```
RESPONSE ::=
  OK | twoErrors | onBoard | full | notOnBoard
OKMessage == [rep!: RESPONSE | rep! = OK]
```

7.7.1   Boarding

A schema to handle errors $BoardError$ is defined. It causes no change to the value of $onboard$, so the schema $ΞAircraft$ is used:

```
┌─ BoardError ──────────────
│ ΞAircraft
│ p?:        PERSON
│ rep!:      RESPONSE
├───────────────────────────
│ (p? ∈ onboard ∧
│ #onboard = capacity ∧
│ rep! = twoErrors)
│ ∨
│ (p? ∈ onboard ∧
│ #onboard < capacity ∧
│ rep! = onBoard)
│ ∨
│ (p? ∉ onboard
│ ∧
│ #onboard = capacity ∧
│ rep! = full)
└───────────────────────────
```

Finally, $Board$ can be defined:

$$Board == (Board_0 \wedge OKMessage) \vee BoardError$$

7.7.2 Disembark

```
┌─ DisembarkError ──────────────────
│ ΞAircraft
│ p?:      PERSON
│ rep!:    RESPONSE
├───────────────────────────────────
│ p? ∉ onboard ∧ rep! = notOnBoard
└───────────────────────────────────
```

Finally *Disembark* can be defined:

$$Disembark == (Disembark_0 \wedge OKMessage) \vee DisembarkError$$

7.8 Example of schemas: Student Programme of Modules

7.8.1 Introduction

This specification concerns a student on a modular course. The student chooses modules from those offered and constructs a *programme* by *adding* and *deleting modules*. The programme is *viable* if it fulfils certain conditions. At least one viable programme must exist.

7.8.2 Types

[MODULE]   the set of all possible modules (module identifications)

7.8.3 Sets

```
┌────────────────────────────────────
│ offered, advanced, basic,
│ field1acc, field2acc: ℙMODULE
├────────────────────────────────────
│ advanced ∩ basic = ∅
│ advanced ∪ basic = offered
│ field1acc ⊆ offered
│ field2acc ⊆ offered
│ #offered ≥ 18
│ #(field1acc ∩ advanced) ≥7
│ #(field2acc ∩ advanced) ≥ 7
│ #((field1acc ∪ field2acc) ∩
│ advanced) ≥ 16
└────────────────────────────────────
```

Certain modules are *offered*. An offered module is either *basic* or *advanced* (not both). Certain offered modules are deemed to be *acceptable* to *field1* and certain to *field2*. A module may be acceptable to more than one field or to none.

For there to be at least one *viable* programme of modules, there must be at least 18 offered modules, at least seven offered that are advanced and acceptable to *field1*, at least seven offered that are advanced and acceptable to *field2*, and at least 16 offered that are advanced and acceptable to the field combination.

The following Venn diagram shows the relationships between the sets in this specification:

Figure 7.1

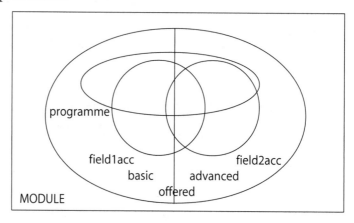

7.8.4 State

The schema *Student* keeps information on the modules in one student's programme. These may only ever be modules that are *offered*.

```
┌─ Student ──────────────────────
│ programme: ℙMODULE
├────────────────────────────────
│ programme ⊆ offered
└────────────────────────────────
```

7.8.5 Initialisation operation

Initially the student has no modules in their programme.

```
┌─ Init ─────────────────────────
│ Student'
├────────────────────────────────
│ programme' = ∅
└────────────────────────────────
```

7.8.6 Operations

Adding a module

```
┌─ Add_0 ────────────────────────────────────
│ ΔStudent
│ m?: MODULE
├────────────────────────────────────────────
│ m? ∈ offered
│ m? ∉ programme
│ programme' = programme ∪ {m?}
└────────────────────────────────────────────
```

The student may only add a module that is offered. The module should not already be in the student's programme. The module is added to the student's programme.

7.8.7 Deleting a module

The module must be in the student's programme. It is deleted from the programme.

```
┌─ Delete_0 ─────────────────────────────────
│ ΔStudent
│ m?: MODULE
├────────────────────────────────────────────
│ m? ∈ programme
│ programme' = programme \ {m?}
└────────────────────────────────────────────
```

7.8.8 Enquiries

$$YESORNO ::= yes \mid no$$

Viable programme

```
┌─ Viable ───────────────────────────────────
│ ΞStudent
│ reply!: YESORNO
├────────────────────────────────────────────
│ (#programme ≥ 18 ∧
│ #(programme ∩ field1acc ∩ advanced) ≥ 7 ∧
│ #(programme ∩ field2acc ∩ advanced) ≥ 7 ∧
│ #(programme ∩ (field1acc ∪ field2acc) ∩ advanced) ≥ 16 ∧
│ reply! = yes)
│ ∨
│ (¬(#programme ≥ 18 ∧
│    #(programme ∩ field1acc ∩ advanced) ≥ 7 ∧
│    #(programme ∩ field2acc ∩ advanced) ≥ 7 ∧
│    #(programme ∩ (field1acc ∪ field2acc) ∩ advanced) ≥ 16) ) ∧
│ reply! = no)
└────────────────────────────────────────────
```

To be viable, the student's programme must have at least 18 offered modules, at least seven offered that are advanced and acceptable to *field1*, at least seven offered that are advanced and acceptable to *field2*, and at least 16 offered that are advanced and acceptable to the field combination.

7.8.9 Error operations

$$RESPONSE ::= OK \mid noSuchModule \mid alreadyRegistered \mid notRegistered$$

7.8.10 Error in adding

```
__AddError_____
  ΞStudent
  m?: MODULE
  resp!: RESPONSE
_____
  (m? ∉ offered ∧ resp! = noSuchModule)
  ∨
  (m? ∈ programme ∧ resp! = alreadyRegistered)
```

If the module is not offered, then the message *noSuchModule* is issued. If the module is already in the programme, then the message *alreadyRegistered* is given. In either case the state remains unchanged.

7.8.11 Error in deleting

```
__DeleteError_____
  ΞStudent
  m?: MODULE
  resp!: RESPONSE
_____
  m? ∉ programme ∧ resp! = notRegistered
```

If the module to be deleted is not in the student's programme, then the message *notRegistered* is given and the state remains unchanged.

7.8.12 Final versions of operations

$$OKMessage ::= [resp!: RESPONSE \mid resp! = OK]$$
$$Add == (Add_0 \wedge OKMessage) \vee AddError$$
$$Delete == (Delete_0 \wedge OKMessage) \vee DeleteError$$

7.8.13 Note

An alternative way of dealing with viability is to construct the set of all *viable programmes*. This will be a set of sets of modules. To say that there must be at least one viable programme it is enough to say that the set of viable programmes is not empty. The section *Sets* can be rewritten:

$$
\begin{array}{l}
\text{offered, advanced, basic,} \\
\text{field1acc, field2acc: } \mathbb{P}\text{MODULE} \\
\text{viableProgrammes : } \mathbb{P}\mathbb{P}\text{MODULE} \\
\hline
\text{advanced} \cap \text{basic} = \varnothing \\
\text{advanced} \cup \text{basic} = \text{offered} \\
\text{field1acc} \subseteq \text{offered} \\
\text{field2acc} \subseteq \text{offered} \\
\text{viableProgrammes} = \{\text{viaProg: } \mathbb{P}\text{MODULE} \mid \\
\quad \#\text{viaProg} \geq 18 \wedge \\
\quad \#(\text{viaProg} \cap \text{field1acc} \cap \text{advanced}) \geq 7 \wedge \\
\quad \#(\text{viaProg} \cap \text{field2acc} \cap \text{advanced}) \geq 7 \wedge \\
\quad \#(\text{viaProg} \cap (\text{field1acc} \cup \text{field2acc}) \cap \text{advanced}) \geq 16 \cdot \text{viaProg}\} \\
\text{viableProgrammes} \neq \varnothing
\end{array}
$$

Now the enquiry *Viable* can just test whether the student's programme is a member of the set of viable programmes:

$$
\begin{array}{l}
\underline{\text{Viable}\hspace{6cm}} \\
\Xi\text{Student} \\
\text{reply!: YESORNO} \\
\hline
(\text{programme} \in \text{viableProgrammes} \wedge \text{reply!} = \text{yes}) \\
\vee \\
(\text{programme} \notin \text{viableProgrammes} \wedge \text{reply!} = \text{no})
\end{array}
$$

EXERCISES

Using the style of this chapter, create the following components of a formal specification for the computer example of Question 1, Chapter 2, and later.

1. The types and the schema for the state.
2. The operation to add a user.
3. The operation to remove a user.
4. The operation to log in.
5. The operation to log out.

CHAPTER 8

Predicates and quantifiers

8.1 Introduction

A *predicate* is a logical statement that depends on a value or values. When a predicate is applied to a particular value it becomes a *proposition*. An example is the predicate:

prime(x)

which depends on some numeric value, x, so that

prime(7)

is a true proposition meaning that seven is a prime number, and

prime(6)

is a false proposition. (A prime number is one that is only divisible by itself and 1).

8.2 Quantifiers

Quantifiers can be applied to predicates to give propositions.

8.2.1 Universal quantifier

The *universal quantifier* is written:

∀

and is pronounced 'for all' (it looks like an upside-down 'A', in *for All*). It is used in the form:

∀ declaration | constraint • predicate

which states that for the declaration(s) given, restricted to certain values (by a predicate called a constraint), the predicate holds.

For each of the quantifiers to be described here, the

| constraint

part may be omitted.

The declaration introduces a typical element that is then optionally constrained. The predicate may apply to this element. For example, to state that all natural numbers less than 10 have squares less than 100:

$$\forall\, i\colon \mathbb{N} \mid i < 10 \bullet i^2 < 100$$

This would be pronounced: 'for all i drawn from the set of natural numbers, such that i is under ten, i squared is less than 100'.

A universal quantification can be thought of as a chain of conjunctions. The quantification above is equivalent to:

$$0^2 < 100 \wedge 1^2 < 100 \wedge \ldots \wedge 8^2 < 100 \wedge 9^2 < 100$$

If the set of values over which the variable is universally quantified is *empty*, then the quantification is defined to be true:

$$\forall\, i\colon \mathbb{N} \mid 0 \le i < 0 \bullet i^2 < 100 \quad \text{is defined to be true}$$

8.2.2 Existential quantifier

The *existential quantifier* is written:

$$\exists$$

and is pronounced 'there exists' (it looks like a backwards 'E', in *there Exists*). It is used in the form:

$$\exists\ \text{declaration} \mid \text{constraint} \bullet \text{predicate}$$

The declaration introduces a typical variable which is then optionally constrained. The predicate applies to this variable. For example, to state that there is a natural number under ten which has a square less than 100:

$$\exists\, i\colon \mathbb{N} \mid i < 10 \bullet i^2 < 100$$

This would be pronounced: 'there exists an i drawn from the set of natural numbers, such that i is less than ten, and i squared is less than 100'.

Note that there need not be only one value of i for which this is true; in this example there are ten: 0 to 9.

To define the predicate *Even*:

$$Even(x) \Leftrightarrow \exists\, k\colon \mathbb{Z} \bullet k * 2 = x$$

A universal quantification can be thought of as a chain of disjunctions.

If the set of values over which the variable is quantified is *empty*, then the existential quantification is defined to be false:

$$\exists\, i\colon \mathbb{N} \mid 0 \le i < 0 \bullet i^2 < 100 \quad \text{is defined to be false}$$

8.2.3 Unique quantifier

The *unique quantifier* is similar to the existential quantifier except that it states that there exists *only one* value for which the predicate is true.

The unique quantifier is written:

$$\exists_1$$

An example is:

$$\exists_1 i: \mathbb{N} \mid i < 10 \bullet i^2 < 100 \wedge i^2 > 80$$

This would be pronounced: 'there exists only one *i* drawn from the set of natural numbers, where *i* is less than ten, such that *i* squared is less than 100 and *i* squared is greater than 80'. It is equivalent to saying that the predicate holds for *i*, but that there is no *j* (with a value different from *i*) for which it holds:

$$\exists_1 i: \mathbb{N} \mid i < 10 \bullet i^2 < 100 \wedge i^2 > 80$$

$$\Leftrightarrow$$

$$\exists i: \mathbb{N} \mid i < 10 \bullet i^2 < 100 \wedge i^2 > 80$$
$$\wedge \neg (\exists j: \mathbb{N} \mid j < 10 \wedge i \neq j \bullet j^2 < 100 \wedge j^2 > 80)$$

8.2.4 Counting quantifier

Some notations use a counting quantifier that counts for how many values of the variable the predicate holds. In Z this is not needed; instead, we use a set comprehension to construct the set of values for which the predicate holds, and then finds the size of the set.

An example is: the number of natural numbers under 10 that have squares greater than 30:

$$\# \{ i: \mathbb{N} \mid i < 10 \bullet i^2 > 30 \}$$

8.2.5 Quantifiers in schema

Quantifiers may be used in the expressions contained in the predicate part of a schema.

8.3 Set comprehension

So far we have given values to sets by listing all their elements. It is also possible to give a value to a set by giving a condition (a *predicate*) which must hold for all members of the set. This can be done by a formulism called a *set comprehension*. The general form is:

$$\{declaration \mid constraint \bullet expression\}$$

▶ The *declaration* is for a typical element and it gives the element's type.

▶ The *constraint* restricts the possible values of the typical element. It is a logical expression which must be true for that value of the typical element to be included.

▶ The *expression* is an expression indicating the value to be included in the set.

A comprehension is very useful for giving a value to an infinite set. For example we cannot write:

$$\{ \ldots -8, -6, -4, -2, 0, 2, 4, 6, 8, \ldots \}$$

since we would then rely on solely the reader's intuition to understand what the continuation indicated by '...' must be. Instead we write:

$$\{x: \mathbb{Z} \mid \text{Even}(x) \cdot x\}$$

Here *x* is the typical value. It is of type *integer* so the set generated will be a *set* of integers. The value of *x* is constrained to be even. The value *x* is included in the generated set. So the generated set is the set of even integers.

The following set comprehension generates the set of the *squares* of the *even* integers:

$$\{x: \mathbb{Z} \mid \text{Even}(x) \cdot x * x\}$$

The constraint and its preceding bar may be omitted:

$$\{x: \mathbb{N} \cdot x * x\} \qquad \text{the squares of the natural numbers}$$

8.3.1 Ranges of numbers

The notation

$$m \mathbin{..} n$$

was introduced in Chapter 2. It is shorthand for

$$\{i: \mathbb{Z} \mid m \leq i \land i \leq n \cdot i\}$$

8.4 Relationship between logic and set theory

There is a direct relationship between some of the operators of logic and operations on sets:

$$[X] \qquad \text{any set}$$
$$S, T: \mathbb{P}X$$
$$S \cup T == \{x: X \mid x \in S \lor x \in T \cdot x\}$$
$$S \cap T == \{x: X \mid x \in S \land x \in T \cdot x\}$$
$$S \setminus T == \{x: X \mid x \in S \land x \notin T \cdot x\}$$

8.5   Summary of notation

$\forall\, x{:}\,T \cdot P$	Universal quantification: 'for all x of type T, P holds'
$\exists\, x{:}\,T \cdot P$	Existential quantification: 'there exists an x of type T, such that P holds'
$\exists_1\, x{:}\,T \cdot P$	Unique existence: 'there exists a unique x of type T, such that P holds'
$\{D \mid P \cdot t\}$	the set of t's declared by D where P holds

EXERCISES

1. Re-express the proposition

    $\forall p{:}\, \text{PERSON} \mid p \in \text{loggedIn} \cdot p \in \text{users}$

    using set relations.

2. Write an expression that states that the squares of all integers are non-negative.

3. Write an expression to state that there is a number that is equal to itself squared.

4. Using the fact that *m mod n* is zero when *m* is divisible by *n* ($m \geq 0$ and $n > 0$) write a set comprehension to define the set of prime numbers.

Relations

9.1 A relation is a set

The examples considered so far have been limited to one basic type which means that the specifications cannot develop to be any more sophisticated. What is needed is some way of relating sets to one another. This can be done by means of a *relation*, which is based on the idea of a *Cartesian product*.

9.2 Cartesian product

A *Cartesian product*, named after the French mathematician Descartes, is a pairing of values of two or more sets. The Cartesian product of the sets or types X, Y and Z would be written:

$$X \times Y \times Z$$

and pronounced 'the Cartesian product of X, Y and Z' or 'X cross Y cross Z'. Values drawn from this combination of sets are called *tuples* and are written:

$$(x, y, z)$$

where x is of type X, y of type Y and z of type Z.

For example:

{red, green} × {hardtop, softtop} =
{(red, hardtop), (red, softtop), (green, hardtop), (green, softtop)}

Such a tuple is called *ordered* since the order of writing the components is important.

A tuple formed from two types is called a *pair* and a tuple formed from three types is called a *triple*. A tuple of n types is sometimes called an *n-tuple*.

An example of a tuple (a 4-tuple) connects information about a person:

NAME × ADDRESS × $\mathbb{N}$ × TELEPHONE

to record name, address, age and telephone-number.

9.3 Relations

A special case of a Cartesian product is a *pair*. A *binary* relation is a set of pairs, of related values.

For example, a relation called *speaks* between countries and languages spoken in those countries can be thought of as a set of pairs. Given:

[COUNTRY]   the set of all countries
[LANGUAGE]   the set of all languages

part of the value of this set might be

{(France, French), (Canada, French),
(Canada, English), (GB, English), (USA, English)}

Figure 9.1

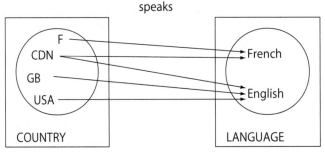

Such a set could be declared:

speaks: $\mathbb{P}$(COUNTRY × LANGUAGE)

Note that there are no restrictions requiring values of the two sets to be paired only one to one; relations pair *many* to *many*. For example, it would be quite acceptable to have the relation:

{(France, French), (Germany, German), (Austria, German),
(Switzerland, French), (Switzerland, German),
(Switzerland, Italian), (Switzerland, Romansch)}

Furthermore, there is no particular reason to choose to relate the values in this direction; one could just as well relate language to country, by declaring:

spoken: $\mathbb{P}$(LANGUAGE × COUNTRY)

9.4 Declaring a relation

The idea of a relation is reinforced by the use of the two-headed arrow in the alternative conventional style of declaration:

R: X ↔ Y
speaks: COUNTRY ↔ LANGUAGE

These can be pronounced: '*R* relates *X* to *Y*' and '*speaks* relates country to language'.

Note the following equivalences:

$$X \leftrightarrow Y == \mathbb{P}(X \times Y)$$

speaks: COUNTRY $\leftrightarrow$ LANGUAGE
==
speaks: $\mathbb{P}$(COUNTRY $\times$ LANGUAGE)

9.5 Maplets

The idea of a related pair is reinforced by the conventional notation for one pair in a relation, a *maplet*:

$$x \mapsto y == (x, y)$$

pronounced '*x* is related to *y*' or '*x* maps to *y*'

GB $\mapsto$ English $\in$ speaks
== (GB, English) $\in$ speaks

The set of pairs given above could alternatively be written as a set of maplets:

{France $\mapsto$ French, Germany $\mapsto$ German, Austria $\mapsto$ German,
Switzerland $\mapsto$ French, Switzerland $\mapsto$ German,
Switzerland $\mapsto$ Italian, Switzerland $\mapsto$ Romansch}

9.6 Membership

To discover if a certain pair of values are related it is sufficient to see if the pair or maplet is an element of the relation:

(GB, English) $\in$ speaks

or

GB $\mapsto$ English $\in$ speaks

9.7 Infix relations

If we declare a relation using low-line characters as place-holders to show the fact that it is *infix*:

speaks: COUNTRY $\leftrightarrow$ LANGUAGE

then we can use the name of the relation as an *infix* operator:

GB speaks English

In general:

$$x \, R \, y == x \mapsto y \in R == (x, y) \in R$$

9.8 Domain and range

A relation relates values of a set called the *source* or *from-set* to values of a set called the *target* or *to-set*. In the example:

R: X $\leftrightarrow$ Y

R = {(x$_1$, y$_2$), (x$_2$, y$_2$), (x$_4$, y$_3$), (x$_6$, y$_3$) , (x$_4$, y$_2$)}

the source is X and the target is Y. In the example:

speaks: COUNTRY $\leftrightarrow$ LANGUAGE

the source is *COUNTRY* and the target is *LANGUAGE*.

9.8.1 Domain

In most cases only a subset of the source is involved in the relation. This subset is called the *domain* and is written *dom*.

In the example the domain of R is

dom R = { x$_1$, x$_2$, x$_4$, x$_6$}

It is the subset containing those values of X which are related by R to values of Y.

9.8.2 Range

Usually only a subset of the target is involved in a relation. This subset is called the *range* and written *ran*.

In the example the range of a relation R is

ran R = {y$_2$, y$_3$}

It is the subset containing those values of Y to which R relates at least one value of X.

Figure 9.2

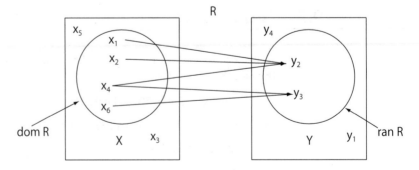

9.8.3 Examples

The domain of the relation *speaks*

> dom speaks

is the set of those countries where at least one language is spoken.
The range of *speaks*

> ran speaks

is that set of languages which are spoken in at least one country.

Figure 9.3

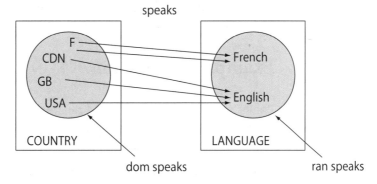

speaks

COUNTRY LANGUAGE

dom speaks ran speaks

9.9 Relational image

To discover the set of values from the range of a relation related to a set of values from the domain of the relation one can use the *relational image*:

> R (S)

pronounced 'the relational image of *S* in *R*'. For example, the languages spoken in France and Switzerland would be:

> speaks ({France, Switzerland})

which is the set

> {French, German, Italian, Romansch}

9.10 Constant value for a relation

Some relations have constant values. If the value of the relation is known, it can be given by an *axiomatic definition*. For example, to define the infix relation greater-than-or-equal-to ($\geq$):

$$\_\geq\_ : \mathbb{Z} \leftrightarrow \mathbb{Z}$$

$$\forall i, j : \mathbb{Z} \bullet i \geq j \Leftrightarrow \exists n : \mathbb{N} \bullet i = j + n$$

Where convenient several relations can be combined in one definition:

$$
\begin{array}{|l}
\_\geq\_: Z \leftrightarrow Z \\
\_>\_: Z \leftrightarrow Z \\
\hline
\forall i, j: Z \bullet \\
(i \geq j \Leftrightarrow \exists n: \mathbb{N} \bullet i = j + n \wedge \\
i > j \Leftrightarrow \exists n: \mathbb{N}_1 \bullet i = j + n)
\end{array}
$$

The low-line (_) characters are used here to indicate that the names ($\geq$) and ($>$) are infix, that is, used between two values.

9.11 Example of a relation

Public holidays around the world can be described as follows:

[COUNTRY]   the set of all the countries of the world
[DATE]   the dates of a given year

The relationship between countries and the dates of the countries' public holidays is the relation *holidays*:

$$
\begin{array}{|l}
\text{Hols} \\
\hline
\text{holidays: COUNTRY} \leftrightarrow \text{DATE}
\end{array}
$$

An operation to discover whether a date *d?* is a public holiday in country *c?* is:

REPLY ::= yes | no

$$
\begin{array}{|l}
\text{Enquire} \\
\hline
\Xi\text{Hols} \\
c?: \qquad \text{COUNTRY} \\
d?: \qquad \text{DATE} \\
rep!: \quad\; \text{REPLY} \\
\hline
(c? \mapsto d? \in \text{holidays} \wedge rep! = \text{yes}) \\
\vee \\
(c? \mapsto d? \notin \text{holidays} \wedge rep! = \text{no})
\end{array}
$$

An operation to decree a public holiday in country *c?* on date *d?* is:

```
  ┌─Decree ─────────────────────────
  │ ΔHols
  │ c?:        COUNTRY
  │ d?:        DATE
  ├─────────────────────────────────
  │ holidays' = holidays ∪ {c? ↦ d?}
  └
```

Note that *Decree* ignores the possibility of the date already being a public holiday in that country.

An operation to abolish a public holiday in country *c?* on date *d?* is:

```
  ┌─Abolish ─────────────────────────
  │ ΔHols
  │ c?:        COUNTRY
  │ d?:        DATE
  ├──────────────────────────────────
  │ holidays' = holidays \ {c? ↦ d?}
  └
```

Note that *Abolish* ignores the possibility of the date not already being a public holiday in that country.

An operation to find the dates *ds!* of all the public holidays in country *c?* is:

```
  ┌─Dates ──────────────────────
  │ ΞHols
  │ c?:        COUNTRY
  │ ds!:       ℙDATE
  ├─────────────────────────────
  │ ds! = holidays ({c?} )
  └
```

9.12 Restriction

Further operators are available to *restrict* a relation.

9.12.1 Domain restriction

The *domain restriction* operator restricts a relation to that part where the domain is contained in a particular set:

$$S \lhd R$$

'the relation R domain restricted to S'.

9.12.2 Range restriction

The *range restriction* operator restricts a relation to that part where the range is contained in a set:

$$R \rhd S$$

'the relation R range restricted to S'.

    The point of the operator can be thought of as pointing right to the range.

9.12.3 Domain subtraction

The domain subtraction operator restricts a relation to that part where the domain is *not* contained in a set:

$$S \ndlhd R$$

'the relation R domain subtracted to S'.

    The point of the operator can be thought of as pointing left to the domain.

9.12.4 Range subtraction

The range subtraction operator restricts a relation to that part where the range is *not* contained in a set:

$$R \ndrhd S$$

'the relation R range subtracted to S'.

9.13 Example of restriction

Given the set of all countries and the set of dates and the relation *holidays* as before and the set of countries in the European Union *EU*

$$EU: \mathbb{P}\,COUNTRY$$

the relation mapping only EU countries to their public holidays is:

$$EU \lhd holidays$$

and the relation mapping *non*-EU countries to their public holidays is:

$$EU \ndlhd holidays$$

Given a subset of dates *summer*

$$summer: \mathbb{P}\,DATE$$

the relation of countries to public holidays in the summer is holidays $\rhd$ summer

and the relation of countries to public holidays *not* in the summer is

holidays $\rhd$ summer

9.14 Composition

Relations can be joined together by an operation called *composition*. Given a relation R which relates X to Y

R: X $\leftrightarrow$ Y

and a relation Q which relates Y to Z

Q: Y $\leftrightarrow$ Z

the following compositions are possible.

9.14.1 Forward composition

The relation formed by the relation R, then the relation Q, is called the *forward composition* of R with Q:

R: X $\leftrightarrow$ Y

Q: Y $\leftrightarrow$ Z

R ; Q: X $\leftrightarrow$ Z

Figure 9.4

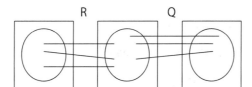

For any pair (x, z) related by R forward composed with Q

x R ; Q z

there is a y where R relates x to y and Q relates y to z:

$\exists$ y: Y • x R y $\wedge$ y Q z

9.14.2 Backward composition

The *backward composition* of Q with R. It is the same as the forward composition of R with Q:

Q $\circ$ R == R ; Q

It is similar to the mathematical notion of *functional composition*.

9.14.3 Repeated composition

A *homogeneous* relation is one which relates values from a type to values of *the same type* (the source and the target are the same). Such a relation can be composed with itself:

$R: X \leftrightarrow X$
$R\,;R: X \leftrightarrow X$

9.15 Example

Countries are related by the relation *borders* if they share a border

borders: COUNTRY $\leftrightarrow$ COUNTRY

For example:

France borders Switzerland
Switzerland borders Austria

Countries are related by *borders* composed with *borders* if they each share a border with a third country

France borders ; borders Austria

since France borders Germany and Germany borders Austria. Note that it is also relates any continental country to itself. (For example, France borders Germany, which borders France.)

The expression:

borders ; borders

can also be written:

France borders^2 Austria

Furthermore:

Spain borders^3 Denmark

means

Spain borders ; borders ; borders Denmark

9.16 Transitive closure

In general, the transitive closure R^+, as used in:

$x\,R^+\,y$

means that there is a repeated composition of R which relates x to y.

For example:

France borders$^+$ India which is true

means that France is on the same land-mass as India.

9.17 Identity relation

The *identity relation*

id X

is the relation which maps all x's on to themselves:

id X == {x: X • x ↦ x}

9.18 Reflexive transitive closure

The repeated composition

= R$^+$ ∪ id X

includes the identity relation. The reflexive transitive closure is similar to the transitive closure except that it includes the identity relation.

x R* x this is always true, even if x R x is false
France borders* France this is true

9.19 Inverse of a relation

The inverse of a relation R from X to Y

R: X ↔ Y

is written

R~

and is the 'mirror image', that is, it relates the same values of Y to X as R relates from X to Y, so if

x R y

then

y R~ x

9.20 Examples

Family relationships can be defined by means of the notation introduced in this chapter.

9.20.1 Definitions

[PERSON]   the set of all persons
father, mother: PERSON $\leftrightarrow$ PERSON

with suitable values and with interpretations:

x father y

and

v mother w

meaning 'x has y as father' and 'v has w as mother'

9.20.2 Parent

The relation *parent* (mother or father)

parent: PERSON $\leftrightarrow$ PERSON

can be defined as the union of the relations *father* and *mother*:

parent = father $\cup$ mother

9.20.3 Sibling

The relation *sibling* (brother or sister)

sibling: PERSON $\leftrightarrow$ PERSON

can be defined as the relation *parent* composed with its own inverse. In other words, the set of persons with the same parents. A person is not usually counted as their own sibling so the identity relation for *PERSON* is excluded:

sibling = (parent ; parent$^{\sim}$) \ id PERSON

9.20.4 Ancestor

The relation *ancestor* can be defined as the repeated composition of *parent*:

ancestor: PERSON $\leftrightarrow$ PERSON
ancestor = parent^{+}

9.21 Summary of notation

X, Y and Z are sets and
x: X;
y: Y;

R: X ↔ Y:

X × Y	the set of ordered pairs of X's and Y's
X ↔ Y	the set of relations from X to Y: $== \mathbb{P}(X \times Y)$
x R y	x is related by R to y: $== (x, y) \in R$
x ↦ y	$== (x, y)$

$\{ x_1 \mapsto y_1, x_2 \mapsto y_2, \ldots, x_n \mapsto y_n \}$

$==$ the relation $\{ (x_1, y_1), (x_2, y_2), \ldots, (x_n, y_n) \}$

relating x_1 to y_1, x_2 to y_2, ..., x_n to y_n

dom R	the domain of a relation
	$== \{x: X \mid (\exists y: Y \bullet x \, R \, y) \bullet x\}$
ran R	the range of a relation
	$== \{y: Y \mid (\exists x: X \bullet x \, R \, y) \bullet y\}$
R (S)	the relational image of S in R
S ◁ R	the relation R domain restricted to S
R ▷ S	the relation R range restricted to S
S ◁ R	the relation R domain anti-restricted to S
R ▷ S	the relation R range anti-restricted to S
R ; Q	the forward composition of R with Q
Q ∘ R	the backward composition of Q with R
id X	$\{x: X \bullet x \mapsto x\}$
R^+	the repeated self-composition of R
R^*	the repeated self-composition of R, with identity
	$== R^+ \cup \text{id } X$
R~	the inverse of R

EXERCISES

In all cases use definitions from this chapter.

1. Express the fact that the language Latin is not spoken in any country (as the official language).

2. Express the fact that Switzerland has four official languages.

3. Give a value to the relation *speaksInEU* which relates countries which are in the set *EU* to their languages.

4. Give a value to the relation *grandparent*.

5. A person's first cousin (or full cousin or cousin-german) is defined as a child of the person's aunt or uncle.

    Give a value for the relation *firstCousin*.

The following questions use these declarations:

[PERSON]	the set of all possible uniquely identified persons
[MODULE]	the set of all module numbers at a university

students, teachers,	
EU, inter:	$\mathbb{P}$PERSON
offered:	$\mathbb{P}$MODULE
studies:	PERSON $\leftrightarrow$ MODULE
teaches:	PERSON $\leftrightarrow$ MODULE

and the predicates:

$EU \cap inter = \varnothing$
$EU \cup inter = students$
$dom\ studies \subseteq students$
$dom\ teaches \subseteq teachers$
$ran\ studies \subseteq offered$
$ran\ teaches = ran\ studies$

6. Explain the *effect* of each of the predicates.
7. Give an expression for the set of modules studied by person p.
8. Give an expression for the *number* of modules taught by person q.
9. Explain what is meant by the *inverse* of the relation *studies*:

    studies~

10. Explain what is meant by the *composition* of relations:

    studies ; teaches~

11. Give an expression for the set of persons who teach person p.
12. Give an expression for the number of persons who teach both person p and person q.
13. Give an expression for that part of the relation *studies* that pertains to international students (those in the set *inter*).
14. Give an expression that states that p and q teach some of the same international students.
15. The following declarations are part of the description of an international conference:

[PERSON]	the set of all possible uniquely identified persons
[LANGUAGE]	the set of languages of the world

    official: $\mathbb{P}$LANGUAGE

    ___CONFERENCE_____
delegates:	$\mathbb{P}$PERSON
official:	$\mathbb{P}$LANGUAGE
speaks:	PERSON $\leftrightarrow$ LANGUAGE

    Write expressions for each of the following (each expression to be independent of the effect of the others):

(a) Every delegate speaks at least one language.

(b) Every delegate speaks at least one official language of the conference.

(c) There is at least one language that every delegate speaks.

(d) There is a delegate who speaks a language that no other delegate speaks.

(e) Write an operation schema to register a new delegate and the set of languages he or she speaks. Include preconditions but do not deal with error conditions.

Functions

10.1 A function is a relation

In a programming language a *function* is a way of specifying some processing which produces a value as a result. In Z a function is a data structure. These two views are not incompatible; the programming language view is just a restricted form of the Z view and in both cases a function provides a result value, given an input value or values.

A function is a special case of a relation in which there is *at most one* value in the range for each value in the domain. A function with a finite domain is also known as a *mapping*.

Figure 10.1

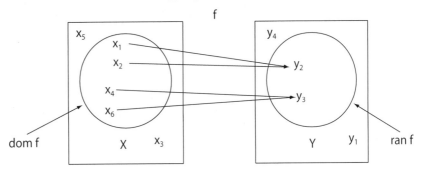

Note that in the diagram the lines do not diverge from left to right. In Z a function f from the type X to the type Y is declared by:

$$f: X \rightarrow Y$$

and is pronounced 'the function f, from X to Y'. This is equivalent to the relation f from X to Y:

$$f : X \leftrightarrow Y$$

with the restriction that for each x in the domain of f, f relates x to *at most one* y:

$$x \in \text{dom } f \Rightarrow \exists_1 y: Y \cdot x f y$$

10.1.1 Examples of functions

The relation between persons and identity numbers:

$$\text{identityNo: PERSON} \leftrightarrow \mathbb{N}$$

is a function if there is a rule that a person may only have one identity number. In this case it would be declared:

identityNo: PERSON $\rightarrowtail$ $\mathbb{N}$

There would probably also be a rule that only one identity number may be associated with any person, but this is not indicated here.

Note that there is no restriction that the function must map different values of the source on to different values of the target. So one could have the function giving a person's mother:

hasMother: PERSON $\rightarrowtail$ PERSON

since any person can have only one mother, but several people may have the same mother.

10.2 Function application

All the concepts which pertain to relations are also applicable to functions. In addition, however, a function may be *applied*. Since there will be at most one value in the range for a given x it is possible to designate that value directly. The value of f applied to x is the value in the range of the function f corresponding to the value x in its domain. The application is undefined if the value of x is not in the domain of f. It is important to check that a value x is in the domain of the function f before attempting to apply f to x.

The application of the function f to the value x (called its *argument*) is written:

f x

and pronounced 'f of x' or 'f applied to x'.

Some people put brackets around the argument, as in:

f(x)

but although this is allowed, it is not necessary.

We check the applicability of f by writing in this style:

$x \in$ dom f
f x = y

10.3 Partial and total functions

The functions given as examples above have been shown as *partial*, which means that there may be values of the source which are not in the domain of the function.

A *total* function is one where there is a value for every possible value of x, so $f x$ is always defined. The domain is the whole of the source. It is declared by f: X → Y

and is pronounced '*f* is a total function from *X* to *Y*'. It is equivalent to the partial function from *X* to *Y* with the restriction that

dom f = X

Because of this, function application can *always* be used with a total function.

10.3.1 Examples of total functions

The function *age*, from *PERSON* to natural numbers, is total since every person has an age:

age: PERSON → ℕ

The function *hasMother*, given above, is total since for any person there is exactly one person who is or was that person's mother:

hasMother: PERSON → PERSON

10.4 Other classes of functions

In addition to total or partial, other classes of functions can be distinguished, as discussed below.

10.4.1 Injection

An *injection*, or *injective function*, is a function which maps different values of the source on to different values of the target.

f: X ↣ Y

The inverse relation of an injective function *f*, from *X* to *Y*, *f*~, is itself a function, from *Y* to *X*:

f~ ∈ Y ↠ X

An injective function may be partial:

f: X ↣ Y

or total:

f: X ↣ Y

Injective functions are sometimes described as 'one-to-one'.
    Since it is likely that each number is associated with only one person, the function *identityNo* given above would be injective. Monogamous

marriage can be expressed as an injective function relating husband to wife (or vice versa).

10.4.2 Surjection

A *surjection*, or *surjective function*, is a function for which its range is the whole of its target. Given the surjective function *f* from *X* to *Y*

ran f = Y

A surjective function may be partial:

f: X $\twoheadrightarrow$ Y

or total:

f: X $\twoheadrightarrow$ Y

Example

Given

SIDE ::= left | right

the function

driveOn: COUNTRY $\twoheadrightarrow$ SIDE   side of the road one drives on

is a *surjection*, because the range includes *all* the values of the type *SIDE*. (There are some countries where one drives on the left and some where one drives on the right). You might consider that it is also *total*, since there are no countries for which the side of the road is not defined:

driveOn: COUNTRY $\twoheadrightarrow$ SIDE

10.4.3 Bijection

A *bijection*, or *bijective function*, is one which maps every element of the source on to every element of the target in a one-to-one relationship. It is therefore: injective, total and surjective:

f: X $\rightarrowtail\!\!\!\rightarrow$ Y

An example of a bijection is a foreign-language vocabulary test that involves finding the pairings between a word in one language and its counterpart in another, where there are to be no left-over words in either list.

10.5 Constant functions

Some functions are used as a means of providing a value, given a parameter or parameters. These are usually functions that maintain a *constant* mapping from their input parameters to their output values. If the value of the mapping is known, a value can be given to the function by an *axiomatic definition*. For example, to define the function *square*:

---

square: $\mathbb{Z} \to \mathbb{N}$

$\forall n: \mathbb{Z} \cdot$
    square n = n * n

Where convenient, several functions can be combined in one definition:

---

square: $\mathbb{Z} \to \mathbb{N}$
cube: $\mathbb{Z} \to \mathbb{Z}$

$\forall n: \mathbb{Z} \cdot$
(square n = n * n $\wedge$
    cube n = n * n * n)

10.6   Overriding

A function or relation can be modified by adding mapping pairs to it or by removing pairs. It can also be modified so that for a particular set of values of the domain it has new values in the range. This is called *overriding*.

For functions or relations *f* and *g*, both of the same type, *f* overridden by *g* is written:

$$f \oplus g$$

It is the same as *f* for all values that are not in the domain of *g*, and the same as *g* for all values that are in the domain of *g*:

If

$$x \in \text{dom } f \wedge x \notin \text{dom } g$$

then

$$f \oplus g \, x = f \, x$$

But if

$$x \in \text{dom } g$$

then

$$f \oplus g \, x = g \, x$$

A definition is:

$$f \oplus g = (\text{dom } g \lhd f) \cup g$$

Note that if *f* and *g* have disjoint domains

$$\text{dom } f \cap \text{dom } g = \varnothing$$

then

$$f \oplus g = f \cup g$$

Example

The recorded age of person *p?* is increased by 1:

$$\text{age} \oplus \{p? \mapsto \text{age } p? + 1\}$$

The function *age* is overridden by the function with only *p?* in its domain which maps *p?* to its former value plus 1.

10.7 Example from business – stock control

A warehouse holds stocks of various items *carried* by an organisation. A computer system records the *level* of all items carried, the *withdrawal* of items from stock and the *delivery* of stock. Occasionally, a new item will be carried and items will be discontinued, provided that their stock level is zero.

[ITEM]   the set of all items (item codes)

```
__Warehouse_____
 carried:  ℙITEM
 level:    ITEM ⇸ ℕ
_____
 dom level = carried
```

Every item carried has a level, even if it is zero.

```
__Init_____
 Warehouse'
_____
 carried' = ∅
 level' = ∅
```

Initially there are no items.

```
__Withdraw_____
 ΔWarehouse
 i?:       ITEM
 qty?:     ℕ₁
_____
 i? ∈ carried
 level i? ≥ qty?
 level' = level ⊕ {i? ↦ (level i? − qty?)}
 carried' = carried
```

For a quantity of an item to be withdrawn, the item must be carried and there must be enough stock.

```
┌─ Deliver ──────────────────────────────
│ ΔWarehouse
│ i?:        ITEM
│ qty?:      ℕ₁
├────────────────────────────────────────
│ i? ∈ carried
│ level' = level ⊕ {i? ↦ (level i? + qty?)}
│ carried' = carried
└────────────────────────────────────────
```

Only deliveries for carried items are accepted. There is no upper limit on stock held.

```
┌─ CarryNewItem ─────────────
│ ΔWarehouse
│ i?:        ITEM
├────────────────────────────
│ i? ∉ carried
│ level' = level ∪ {i? ↦ 0}
│ carried' = carried ∪ {i?}
└────────────────────────────
```

A new item must not already be carried and will initially have a level of zero.

```
┌─ DiscontinueItem ──────────
│ ΔWarehouse
│ i?:        ITEM
├────────────────────────────
│ i? ∈ carried
│ level i? = 0
│ carried' = carried \ {i?}
│ level' = {i?} ⊲ level
└────────────────────────────
```

An item to be discontinued must currently be carried and must have a level of zero.

Note: errors have not been handled in this simple version.

10.8 Example from data processing

10.8.1 Indexed-sequential files

In the programming language COBOL a type of data file called an indexed-sequential file is available. In principle an indexed-sequential file is a sequence of records which can be accessed in any order by specifying the value of a field of the desired record, called the *key*. There is at most one record in the file for any value of the key.

Operations are available to read, write, insert and delete records (using the COBOL instructions *READ*, *REWRITE*, *WRITE* and *DELETE* respectively). The behaviour of these operations can be specified as follows:

[KEY] set of all keys for this file
[DATA] remaining fields of record (other than key)

```
┌─ISFile────────────────
│ file:    KEY ⇸ DATA
│
```

The file is regarded as a function from a *key* to the rest of the *data* in the record. The function is partial since there may be values of the key for which there is no record on the file.

10.8.2 Read operation

The operation *Read* is a function application:

```
┌─Read────────────────────
│ ΞISFile
│ k?:       KEY
│ result!:  DATA
├─────────────────────────
│ k? ∈ dom file
│ result! = file k?
│
```

The value of *result!* is the data of the record with the key *k?*, if there is one. The first line of the predicate is to check the applicability of the function *file* to the given key. The file is unchanged.

10.8.3 Rewrite operation

The operation *Rewrite* is a functional overriding:

```
┌─Rewrite──────────────────
│ ΔISFile
│ k?:     KEY
│ new?:   DATA
├──────────────────────────
│ k? ∈ dom file
│ file' = file ⊕ {k? ↦ new?}
│
```

The function is changed only for the value of *k?* in the domain, which now maps to the new data *new?*.

10.8.4 Write operation

The operation *Write* is a functional (relational) union:

```
┌─ Write ──────────────────
│ ΔISFile
│ k?:      KEY
│ new?:    DATA
├──────────────────────────
│ k? ∉ dom file
│ file' = file ∪ {k? ↦ new?}
└──────────────────────────
```

10.8.5 Delete operation

The operation *Delete* is a functional (relational) domain anti-restriction:

```
┌─ Delete ─────────────────
│ ΔISFile
│ k?:      KEY
├──────────────────────────
│ k? ∈ dom file
│ file' = {k?} ◁ file
└──────────────────────────
```

10.8.6 Error conditions

The handling of errors has not been included here, to keep the specification simple. The schemas could easily be extended to include a report of success or failure.

10.8.7 Further facilities

The COBOL language allows further operations on indexed-sequential files which make use of the fact that the records of such a file are held in order (ordered on the key). Clearly, the specification used above would not suffice to specify those operations. However, it gives a very concise explanation of the simple operations.

10.9 Summary of notation

$X \nrightarrow Y$ the set of partial functions from X to Y:
$$== \{ f: X \leftrightarrow Y \mid (\forall x: X \mid x \in \text{dom } f \bullet (\exists_1 y: Y \bullet x f y)) \bullet f \}$$

$X \rightarrow Y$ the set of total functions from X to Y:
$$== \{ f: X \nrightarrow Y \mid \text{dom } f = X \bullet f \}$$

$X \rightarrowtail Y$ the set of partial injective functions from X to Y:
$$== \{ f: X \nrightarrow Y \mid f^{\sim} \in Y \nrightarrow X \bullet f \}$$

$X \rightarrowtail Y$ the set of total injective functions from X to Y:
$$== \{ f: X \rightarrowtail Y \mid \text{dom } f = X \bullet f \}$$

$X \nrightarrow\!\!\!\!\to Y$ the partial surjective functions from X to Y:
$$== \{ f: X \nrightarrow Y \mid \text{ran } f = Y \}$$

$X \rightarrow\!\!\!\!\to Y$ the total surjective functions from X to Y:
$$== \{ f: X \nrightarrow\!\!\!\!\to Y \mid \text{dom } f = X \}$$

$X \rightarrowtail\!\!\!\!\to Y$ the bijective functions from X to Y
(total, injective and surjective)
$$== (X \rightarrow Y) \cap (X \rightarrowtail Y)$$

$f x$ *or* $f(x)$ the function f applied to x

$f \oplus g$ functional overriding
$$== (\text{dom } g \vartriangleleft f) \cup g$$

EXERCISES

1. A system records the bookings of hotel rooms on one night.
    Given the basic types:

[ROOM]	the set of all the rooms in the hotel
[PERSON]	the set of all possible persons

    the state of the hotel's bookings can be represented by the following schema:

    ┌─ Hotel ─────────────────────────
    │ bookedTo: ROOM $\nrightarrow$ PERSON
    └─────────────────────────────────

    (a) Explain why *bookedTo* is a *function*.
    (b) Explain why the function is *partial*.

2. An initialisation operation is:

```
┌─ Init ─────────────────────────
│  Hotel'
│ ───────────────────────────────
│  bookedTo' = ∅
└────────────────────────────────
```

and a first version of the operation to accept a booking is:

```
┌─ AcceptBooking₀ ─────────────────
│  ΔHotel
│  p?:      PERSON
│  r?:      ROOM
│ ─────────────────────────────────
│  r? ∉ dom bookedTo
│  bookedTo' = bookedTo ∪ {r? ↦ p?}
└───────────────────────────────────
```

Explain the meaning and purpose of each line of the schema above.

3. Write a schema $CancelBooking_0$ which cancels a booking made for a given person and a given room. It should deal with error conditions in the same manner as $AcceptBooking_0$.

4. Explain the meaning and purpose of each line of your schema $CancelBooking_0$.

5. The following partially specifies the Olympic games in held Sydney in the year 2000:

[COUNTRY]   the set of all countries of the world
[PERSON]   the set of all uniquely identified persons
[EVENT]   the set of all sporting events

```
┌─ Sydney2000 ─────────────────────────────
│  participating:   ℙCOUNTRY
│  events:          ℙEVENT
│  represents:      PERSON ↔ COUNTRY
│  competesIn:      PERSON ↔ EVENT
│  won:             EVENT ↔ PERSON
│ ──────────────────────────────────────────
│  ???
└────────────────────────────────────────────
```

A person can only represent one participating country. A person can only compete in an event if he or she is representing a country and if the event is one of those of the Sydney 2000 games. Only one of the competitors in an event can win it.

(a) All the relationships have been given as general relations. Consider which of these might be better specified as functions. Re-write the signature of the schema *Sydney2000* showing this and justify your changes.

(b) Consider the relationships between the variables of your schema *Sydney2000* and add predicates to represent these. Justify your predicates.

(c) Write a schema *JoinGames* which records a new country joining in the Sydney games.

(d) Write a schema *Win* that records the winner of an event.

(e) Write a schema *CountryGolds* that supplies the number of events that have been won by representatives of a given country.

A seat allocation system

11.1 Introduction

This example concerns recording the allocation of seats to passengers on an aircraft.

11.2 The types

The types involved here are the set of *all possible* persons, called *PERSON*, and the set of all seats *on this aircraft*, *SEAT*.

[PERSON]	the set of all possible uniquely identified persons
[SEAT]	the set of all seats on this aircraft

11.3 The state

The state of the system is given by the relation between the set of seats and the set of persons:

```
┌─ Seating ─────────────────────────────
│  bookedTo:      SEAT ⇸ PERSON
└───────────────────────────────────────
```

Note that a seat may be booked to only one person, but a person may book many seats.

11.4 Initialisation operation

There must be an initial state for the system. The obvious one is where the aircraft is entirely unbooked. An initialisation operation is:

```
┌─ Init ──────────────────────
│  Seating'
│ ────────────────────────────
│  bookedTo' = ∅
└─────────────────────────────
```

11.5 Operations

11.5.1 Booking

There is an operation to allow a person $p?$, to book the seat $s?$. A first attempt is:

```
┌─ Book₀ ────────────────────────────
│ ΔSeating
│ p?:        PERSON
│ s?:        SEAT
├────────────────────────────────────
│ s? ∉ dom bookedTo
│ bookedTo' = bookedTo ∪ {s? ↦ p?}
└────────────────────────────────────
```

11.5.2 Cancel

It is also necessary to have an operation to allow a person $p?$ to cancel a booking for a seat $s?$:

```
┌─ Cancel₀ ──────────────────────────
│ ΔSeating
│ p?:        PERSON
│ s?:        SEAT
├────────────────────────────────────
│ s? ↦ p? ∈ bookedTo
│ bookedTo' = bookedTo \ { s? ↦ p?}
└────────────────────────────────────
```

11.6 Enquiry operations

These operations leave the state unchanged.

11.6.1 Whose seat

In addition to operations which change the state of the system it is necessary to have an operation to discover the owner of a seat:

REPLY ::= yes | no

```
┌─ WhoseSeat ────────────────────┐
│ ΞSeating                       │
│ s?:       SEAT                 │
│ taken!:   REPLY                │
│ who!:     PERSON               │
├────────────────────────────────┤
│ (s? ∈ dom bookedTo ∧           │
│ taken! = yes ∧                 │
│ who! = bookedTo s? )           │
│ ∨                              │
│ (s? ∉ dom bookedTo ∧           │
│ taken! = no)                   │
└────────────────────────────────┘
```

11.7 Dealing with errors

The schemas $Book_0$ and $Cancel_0$ do not state what happens if their preconditions are not satisfied. The schema calculus of Z allows these schemas to be extended, firstly to give a message in the event of success:

RESPONSE ::= OK | alreadyBooked | notYours
OKMessage == [rep!: RESPONSE | rep! = OK]

11.7.1 Booking

A schema to handle errors on making a booking is defined:

```
┌─ BookError ────────────────────┐
│ ΞSeating                       │
│ s?:       SEAT                 │
│ p?:       PERSON               │
│ rep!:     RESPONSE             │
├────────────────────────────────┤
│ s? ∈ bookedTo                  │
│ rep! = alreadyBooked           │
└────────────────────────────────┘
```

Finally, *Book* can be defined:

Book == (Book$_0$ ∧ OKMessage) ∨ BookError

11.7.2 Cancel

A schema to handle errors on cancelling a booking is defined:

$$\begin{array}{|l}
\underline{\text{CancelError}} \qquad\qquad\qquad \\
\;\Xi\text{Seating} \\
\;\text{s?:} \qquad \text{SEAT} \\
\;\text{p?:} \qquad \text{PERSON} \\
\;\text{rep!:} \qquad \text{RESPONSE} \\
\hline
\;\text{s?} \mapsto \text{p?} \notin \text{bookedTo} \\
\;\text{rep!} = \text{notYours}
\end{array}$$

Finally *Cancel* can be defined:

$$\text{Cancel} == (\text{Cancel}_0 \wedge \text{OKMessage}) \vee \text{CancelError}$$

EXERCISES

By using schema inclusion where possible, extend your specification of the computer system from Question 1, Chapter 2, and onwards, to include security passwords. Each registered user must have a password. On being registered a user is given a dummy password. Use the declarations:

PASSWORD   the set of all possible passwords
dummy: PASSWORD

1. Give a schema to define the state of this system.
2. Give an initialisation operation for the system.
3. Give a schema for the operation to register a new user.
4. Give a schema for the operation to log in. The user must give the correct password. Consider only the case where the user gives the correct password.
5. Give a schema for a logged-in user to change the password. The user must supply the new and the old passwords. Define only the case where the conditions are met.

Sequences

12.1 A sequence is a function

Very often it is necessary to be able to distinguish values of a set by position or to permit duplicate values or to impose some ordering on the values. For this a *sequence* is the appropriate structure.

A sequence of elements of type X is regarded in Z as a function from the natural numbers to elements of X. The domain of the function is defined to be the interval of the natural numbers starting from one and going up to the number of elements in the sequence, with no gaps.

A sequence s of elements of type X is declared:

   s: seq X

and is equivalent to declaring the function:

   $s: \mathbb{N} \nrightarrow X$

with the constraint that:

   dom s = 1 .. #s

12.2 Sequence constructors

A sequence constant can be constructed by listing its elements in order, enclosed by special angle brackets and separated by commas:

   [CITY]   the set of cities of the world
   flight: seq CITY

   flight = ⟨ Geneva, Paris, London, NewYork ⟩

This is a shorthand for the function:

   flight = {1 ↦ Geneva, 2 ↦ Paris, 3 ↦ London, 4 ↦ NewYork}

The order of cities in *flight* might be the order in which those cities are visited on a journey starting in Geneva and finishing in New York.

12.2.1 The length of a sequence

The length of a sequence s is simply the size of the function

   #s

so

$$\#flight = 4$$

12.2.2 Empty sequence

The sequence with no elements is written as empty sequence brackets:

$$\langle\, \rangle$$

12.2.3 Non-empty sequences

If a sequence may never be empty, that is, it must always have at least one element, it can be declared:

$s: \text{seq}_1 X$

which is the same as defining

$s: \text{seq } X$

and adding the constraint

$\#s > 0$

12.3 Sequence operators

12.3.1 Selection

Since a sequence is a function, it is possible to select an element by position simply by function application. For example, to select the third element of *flight*:

flight 3   this is London

As with a function, it only makes sense to attempt to select with a value which is in the domain of the function. In terms of the sequence, that means the position value must be between one and the number of elements in the sequence.

12.3.2 Head

The *head* of a sequence is its first element, so

head flight

is the same as

flight 1   this is Geneva

12.3.3 Tail

The *tail* of a sequence is the sequence with its head removed, so

> tail flight

is the sequence

> ⟨ Paris, London, NewYork ⟩

12.3.4 Last

The *last* of a sequence is its last element, so

> last flight

is the same as

> flight #flight   this is NewYork

12.3.5 Front

The *front* of a sequence is the sequence with its last element removed, so

> front flight

is the sequence

> ⟨ Geneva, Paris, London ⟩

12.3.6 Concatenation

The *concatenation* operator is written

> ⌢

and pronounced 'concatenated with' or 'catenated with'. It chains together two sequences to form a new sequence. For example:

> ⟨ Geneva, Paris, London, NewYork ⟩ ⌢ ⟨ Seattle, Tokyo ⟩

is the sequence

> ⟨ Geneva, Paris, London, NewYork, Seattle, Tokyo ⟩

12.3.7 Filtering

The operation of *filtering* a sequence produces a new sequence, all of whose elements are members of a specified set. Its effect is similar to that of performing a range restriction, then 'squashing up' the elements to close up the gaps left by omitted elements. For example:

> flight ↾ {London, Geneva, Rome}

is pronounced 'flight filtered by the set containing London, Geneva and Rome' and results in the sequence:

⟨ London, Geneva ⟩

Note that the ordering remains that of the original sequence.
To form the sequence of those cities of *flight* which are in Europe given:

EuropeanCities: PCITY
EuropeanCities = {Paris, London, Geneva, Rome}

we can write:

flight ↾ EuropeanCities

which is

⟨ Geneva, Paris, London ⟩

12.3.8   Restriction and squash

Since a sequence is a function and a function is a relation, the relational operators can be used. The relational restriction operators are particularly useful; for example, to select parts of a sequence.
Given:

S: seq X

then

1..n ◁ S

is the sequence of the first *n* elements of *S*.
In general, a restriction of a sequence *does not* yield a *sequence*, since the resulting domain will not be of contiguous natural numbers starting at one. In that case the special operator *squash* can be used to convert the relation into a sequence by 'closing up the gaps'.
So:

squash (m .. n ◁ S)

is the *sequence* of the elements from position *m* to position *n* of *S*. Note that *squash* only works for functions where the domain is the natural numbers.
The sequence filtering

flight ↾ EuropeanCities

is equivalent to

squash (flight ▷ EuropeanCities)

12.3.9 Reversing a sequence

The operator

> rev

reverses the order of elements in a sequence. For example

> rev flight = ⟨ NewYork, London, Paris, Geneva ⟩

12.3.10 Range

Since a sequence is just a special case of a function, it is permissible, and sometimes useful, to refer to the *range* of a sequence; that is, the *set* of values which appear in the sequence. For example:

> ran flight = {Geneva, Paris, London, NewYork}

12.4 Example of using sequences – stack

The well known and widely used data structure called a *stack* can be defined by means of sequences.

A stack is a data structure into which elements can be added ('pushed') and removed ('popped'). The next element to be popped is the one most recently pushed. This behaviour is also explained by referring to this as a *last-in-first-out* structure.

12.4.1 Types

The general type X is used:

> [X]   any type

12.4.2 The state

```
┌─ Stack ──────────────────┐
│  s:       seq X          │
│                          │
└──────────────────────────┘
```

12.4.3 The initialisation operation

```
┌─ Init ───────────────────┐
│  Stack'                  │
├──────────────────────────┤
│  s' = ⟨ ⟩                │
└──────────────────────────┘
```

Initially the sequence *s* is empty.

12.4.4 Push

A new element will be added at the front of the sequence:

```
┌─ Push ─────────────────────
│ ΔStack
│ x?:        X
├────────────────────────────
│ s' = ⟨x?⟩ ⌢ s
└────────────────────────────
```

Note that the new value could just as well have been added at the back of the sequence, so long as *Pop* then had the appropriate definition.

12.4.5 Pop

An element will be removed from the front of the sequence:

```
┌─ Pop ──────────────────────
│ ΔStack
│ x!:        X
├────────────────────────────
│ s ≠ ⟨ ⟩
│ x! = head s
│ s' = tail s
└────────────────────────────
```

The precondition of *Pop* is that the sequence *s* should not be empty.
An alternative definition of *Pop*, which shows its symmetry with *Push*, is:

```
┌─ Pop ──────────────────────
│ ΔStack
│ x!:        X
├────────────────────────────
│ s ≠ ⟨ ⟩
│ s = ⟨x!⟩ ⌢ s'
└────────────────────────────
```

12.4.6 Length

The *length* of the stack is the length of the sequence.

```
┌─ Length ───────────────────
│ ΞStack
│ len!:       ℕ
├────────────────────────────
│ len! = # s
└────────────────────────────
```

12.5 Example of using sequences – an air route

A route to be taken by a passenger on a journey by air can be described by the sequence of airports that the passenger will pass through. For the proposed journey to be viable, adjacent airports on the route must be connected by air services.

[AIRPORT]   the set of airports in the world

```
__AirServices_____
  _connected_: AIRPORT ↔ AIRPORT
_____
```

An operation to propose a viable route from the originating to the destination airport might be:

```
__ProposeRoute_____
  ΞAirServices
  from?, to?:    AIRPORT
  route!:        seq AIRPORT
  _____
  head route! = from?
  last route! = to?
  (∀ changePos: ℕ |
  changePos ∈ 1..#route! – 1 •
  route changePos connected
  route changePos + 1)
_____
```

Of course, there may in fact not be a viable route between any two airports.

Note that this operation does not rule out providing a route which goes through the same airport more than once, and even allows flights which land back where they started. Since it seems unlikely that passengers would wish to fly more legs on their journeys than necessary, a better version would eliminate such excessively long routes:

```
__NoDuplicatesRoute_____
  ProposeRoute
  _____
  (∀ i, j: ℕ |
  {i, j} ⊆ 1..#route! •
  i ≠ j ⇒ route i ≠ route j)
_____
```

This says that for any *i* and *j* within the domain of the function (legal positions), if *i* and *j* are different, then so are the values in the sequence at positions *i* and *j*.

An alternative way of stating that no duplicates are permitted is to require that the inverse of the sequence be a function:

```
┌─ NoDuplicatesRoute ──────────────
│ ProposeRoute
│ ───────────────────────────────
│ route~ ∈ AIRPORT ⇸ ℕ
└──────────────────────────────────
```

or simply to state that:

$$\#route = \#ran\ route$$

12.6 Sequences with no duplicates permitted

To specify that there are to be no duplicates in a sequence is a common requirement and so, for convenience, a special declaration of an *injective* sequence can be used.

iseq X

is the set of sequences of X's where no value of X appears more than once in the sequence.

```
┌─ NoDuplicatesRoute ──────────────────────
│ ΞAirServices
│ from?, to?:          AIRPORT
│ route!:              iseq AIRPORT
│ ────────────────────────────────────────
│ head route! = from?
│ last route! = to?
│ #route = #ran route
│ (∀ changePos: ℕ |
│   changePos ∈ 1..#route! − 1 •
│   route changePos connected
│   route changePos + 1)
└──────────────────────────────────────────
```

12.7 Example of using sequences – files in Pascal

In the programming language Pascal a file is a sequential structure of some type of elements. A file can be either in *inspection* mode or in *generation* mode. The file is put into inspection mode by a *Reset* operation and when in inspection mode can be read from by a *Read* operation. The file is put into *generation* mode by a *Rewrite* operation which makes the file empty. When in *generation* mode the file can have new elements appended to it by a *Write* operation.

This specification ignores buffering of data.

> [X]   any type of data (some restrictions in Pascal)
> FILEMODE ::= inspection | generation

12.7.1 The file state

```
┌─ PascalFile ──────────────────────
│  file:            seq X
│  stillToRead:     seq X
│  mode:            FILEMODE
│ ─────────────────────────────────
│  ∃ alreadyRead: seq X •
│  alreadyRead ⌢ stillToRead = file
└───────────────────────────────────
```

The part of the file still to be read is always a *suffix* of the whole file.

12.7.2 The Reset operation

```
┌─ Reset ──────────────────
│  ΔPascalFile
│ ─────────────────────────
│  mode' = inspection
│  stillToRead' = file
│  file' = file
└──────────────────────────
```

The mode is switched to inspection and the whole of the file is still to be read. The content of the file is not changed by this operation.

12.7.3 The Read operation

```
┌─ Read ────────────────────────────
│  ΔPascalFile
│  x!:        X
│ ─────────────────────────────────
│  mode = inspection
│  stillToRead ≠ ⟨ ⟩
│  ⟨ x! ⟩ ⌢ stillToRead' = stillToRead
│  file' = file
│  mode' = mode
└───────────────────────────────────
```

The mode must be inspection; the part of the file still to be read must not be empty. The value returned is taken from the front of the part of the file still to be read. The file and its mode are unchanged.

12.7.4   The Rewrite operation

```
┌─ Rewrite ──────────────────
│ ΔPascalFile
├────────────────────────────
│ mode' = generation
│ file' = ⟨ ⟩
└────────────────────────────
```

The mode is switched to generation and the file becomes empty.

12.7.5   The Write operation

```
┌─ Write ────────────────────
│ ΔPascalFile
│ x?:        X
├────────────────────────────
│ mode = generation
│ file' = file ⌢ ⟨ x? ⟩
│ mode' = mode
└────────────────────────────
```

The mode must be generation. The value to be written is appended to the file. The mode is unchanged.

12.7.6   End of file

End of file is true when the part of the file still to be read is an empty sequence

$$stillToRead = ⟨ ⟩$$

12.8   Summary of notation

seq X	the set of sequences whose elements are drawn from X $== \{S: \mathbb{N} \nrightarrow X \mid dom\ S = 1 .. \#S\}$
seq_1 X	set of non-empty sequences
iseq X	set of injective sequences (no duplicates)
#S	the length of the sequence S
⟨ ⟩	the empty sequence { }
$⟨x_1, ... x_n⟩$	$== \{1 \mapsto x_1, ..., n \mapsto x_n\}$

$$\langle x_1, \ldots x_n \rangle \,^\frown \langle y_1, \ldots y_n \rangle$$

concatenation:

$$== \langle x_1, \ldots x_n, y_1, \ldots y_n \rangle$$

head S	$== S\,1$
last S	$== S\,\#S$
tail $(\langle x \rangle \,^\frown S)$	$== S$
front $(S \,^\frown \langle x \rangle)$	$== S$
squash f	the function f (f: $\mathbb{N} \rightarrow X$) squashed into a sequence
S ↾ s	the sequence S filtered to elements in s
	$==$ squash $(S \rhd s)$
rev S	the sequence S in reverse order

EXERCISES

1. Given the sequences of cities:

    u, v: seq CITY

   and the values

    u = ⟨ London, Amsterdam, Madrid ⟩

   and

    v = ⟨ Paris, Frankfurt ⟩

   write down the values of the sequences:

    u ⌢ v
    rev (u ⌢ v)
    rev u
    rev v
    rev v ⌢ rev u

2. Referring to Question 1, find the value of

    squash (2 .. 4 ◁ rev (u ⌢ v))

3. Find the value of

    squash (4 .. 2 ◁ rev (u ⌢ v))

4. Find the value of

    u ⌢ v ↾ { London, Moscow, Paris, Rome }

5. Find the value of

    tail (u ⌢ v) ⌢ front ⟨ Moscow, Berlin, Warsaw ⟩

113

The following questions use these declarations:

[CHAR]   the set of all possible characters

```
┌─ TEXT ─────────────────────
│ stream:  seq CHAR
│
```

```
┌─ P ──────────────────────────────────────────────
│ ΞTEXT:
│ pat?:     seq CHAR
│ pos!:     ℕ
├──────────────────────────────────────────────────
│ ((∃ before, after: seq CHAR • before ⌢ pat? ⌢ after = stream) ∧
│ pos! = #before + 1)
│   ∨
│ (¬(∃ before, after: seq CHAR • before ⌢ pat? ⌢ after = stream) ∧
│ pos! = 0)
│
```

6. Explain the meaning of each line of and the overall effect of the schema *P*.

7. Write a schema *Delete* which deletes the *first* occurrence of the subsequence *pat?* from the stream and sets *pos!* to the start position of the subsequence (or to zero if the subsequence was not found).

13

An example of sequences – the aircraft example again

13.1 Introduction

A system can be specified in terms of sequences. This chapter shows the aircraft example done in this fashion. Usually it is harder to use sequences; they are much less abstract than sets since order must be taken into account. A process called *refinement* concerns producing a more concrete specification from an abstract one. In so doing each transformation can be shown to be a correct implementation of its (more abstract) specification.

13.2 The state

The passengers' identifications are held in a sequence, which does not contain any name more than once:

```
┌─ SeqAircraft ──────────────
│
│  passengers: iseq PERSON
│  ─────────────────────────
│  #passengers ≤ capacity
│
```

The relationship (the *abstraction function, ABS*) between the abstract specification *Aircraft* and the more concrete *SeqAircraft* is given by:

```
┌─ ABS ──────────────────────
│
│  Aircraft
│  SeqAircraft
│  ─────────────────────────
│  onboard = ran passengers
│
```

13.3   Initialisation operation

The sequence is empty:

```
┌─ SeqInit ─────────────────────────
│  SeqAircraft'
│ ─────────────────────────────────
│  passengers' = ⟨ ⟩
└───────────────────────────────────
```

13.4   Operations

13.4.1   Boarding

The new person is appended to (the end of) the sequence:

```
┌─ SeqBoard ────────────────────────
│  p?:        PERSON
│  ΔSeqAircraft
│ ─────────────────────────────────
│  p? ∉ ran passengers
│  #passengers < capacity
│  passengers' = passengers ⌢ ⟨p?⟩
└───────────────────────────────────
```

13.4.2   Disembark

```
┌─ SeqDisembark ────────────────────
│  p?:        PERSON
│  ΔSeqAircraft
│ ─────────────────────────────────
│  p? ∈ ran passengers
│  (∃ before, after: iseq PERSON •
│  passengers = before ⌢ ⟨p?⟩ ⌢ after ∧
│  passengers' = before ⌢ after)
└───────────────────────────────────
```

Note how much more complex this is than the set-based version; the element must be removed from the right place in the sequence.

13.5 Enquiry operations

13.5.1 Number on board

```
┌─ SeqNumber ─────────────────
│ numOnboard!:   ℕ
│ ΞSeqAircraft
├─────────────────────────────
│ numOnboard! = #passengers
└─────────────────────────────
```

The number on board is the length of the sequence, since there are no duplicates.

13.5.2 Person on board

REPLY ::= yes | no

```
┌─ SeqOnBoard ─────────────────
│ p?:      PERSON
│ rep!:    REPLY
│ ΞSeqAircraft
├──────────────────────────────
│ (p? ∈ ran passengers ∧
│ rep = yes)
│ ∨
│ (p? ∉ ran passengers ∧
│ rep = no)
└──────────────────────────────
```

13.6 Dealing with errors

For the sake of simplicity the sections on dealing with errors have been omitted here.

13.7 Implementation

Since a sequence is easily modelled in a programming language, either by the language's sequence type in the case of an applicative language, or by files or arrays in a procedural language, a sequence is closer to being implementable than, say, a set or a relation, and is thus regarded as being more concrete. In a complex specification it is best to start with a simpler, more abstract specification, in terms of sets, functions and so on, and to refine this later to a more concrete, equivalent specification. This process of refinement is itself the subject of books.

EXERCISES

1. Define a schema for the state of a system which will maintain a *file* which is a sequence of *bytes*.
2. Give a schema for a suitable initialisation operation.
3. Give a schema for an operation to *insert* a sequence of bytes *after* a given position in the file.
4. Give a schema to *delete* the sequence of bytes within the file, given suitable starting and ending positions.
5. Give a schema to *copy* a sequence of bytes within the file, given the starting and ending positions, into an output *buffer*.

Extending a specification

14.1 Limitations of specifications given so far

The most complex specification given so far in this book concerns booking of seats on an aircraft. This example is unrealistic in that it only considers one flight of one aircraft. It is wise to start a specification in this way by simplifying the problem, but naturally it would be useful to extend this specification to consider many flights.

14.2 The type of a flight

The new type *FLIGHT* will be introduced for this extended specification.

[FLIGHT]   the set of all flight identifications

If the flight identification is composed of a date and a flight number it could be declared as:

[DATE]   the set of all dates
[FLIGHTNO]   the set of all flight numbers

FLIGHT == DATE × FLIGHTNO

The twin equal signs mean abbreviation definition.

14.3 A function to a function

The behaviour of the extended system of seat bookings across a fleet of aircraft is to be the same for each flight, so the new seat booking information can conveniently be represented by a function from flight to seat bookings for that flight. The seat bookings for a flight will be, as before, a function from seat to person.

[SEAT]   the set of all seat numbers
[PERSON]   the set of all persons

The state schema will use the function *booked*:

booked: FLIGHT $\nrightarrow$ (SEAT $\nrightarrow$ PERSON)

Note that for any flight f

booked f

is a function from *SEAT* to *PERSON*, as in the previous, simpler, version of this specification and, for any seat s

booked f s

is the application of the function from *SEAT* to *PERSON* yielded by the application of the function *booked* to the flight f, and is thus the person to whom the seat s on flight f is booked.

14.3.1 Seats and aircraft

It is no longer sufficient to consider the set *SEAT* to be the set of seats on this aircraft, since there are now several aircraft involved and the available seat numbers will vary according to the aircraft type. For this reason *SEAT* has been declared as the set of *all* seat *numbers* and a new function *hasSeat* is used to discover what seat numbers a flight has assigned to it.

The relating of a seat to a flight rather than to a particular aircraft reflects the fact that the same seat number on a given aircraft can be booked many times in its lifetime, but only once for a given flight of that aircraft.

14.4 The state

Only the seat numbers assigned to a flight may be booked.

FleetSeatAllocation

booked: FLIGHT $\nrightarrow$ (SEAT $\nrightarrow$ PERSON)
hasSeat: FLIGHT $\leftrightarrow$ SEAT

---
dom booked = dom hasSeat
$\forall$ f: FLIGHT | f $\in$ dom booked •
dom (booked f) $\subseteq$ hasSeat ({f})

Figure 14.1

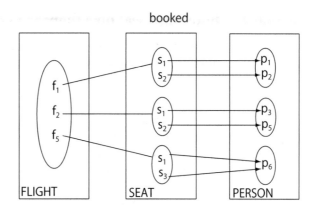

booked

14.5   Initialisation operation

A possible initial state is where there are no bookings for any seats on any
flights.

```
Init
  FleetSeatAllocation'
  ────────────────────
  hasSeat' = Ø
  booked' = Ø
```

14.6   Operations

14.6.1   Creating a new flight

An operation to create a new flight is

```
NewFlight₀
  ΔFleetSeatAllocation
  f?:              FLIGHT
  available?:      ℙSEAT
  ─────────────────────────────────────────────────
  f? ∉ dom booked
  available? ≠ Ø
  hasSeat' = hasSeat ∪ {s: SEAT | s ∈ available? • f? ↦ s}
  booked' = booked ∪ {f? ↦ Ø}
```

The flight must not already be known. The set of seats available to that
flight must not be empty. The seat bookings for the new flight are initially
empty.

14.6.2 Booking a seat on a flight

An operation to book a seat on a particular flight needs to have flight, seat number and person as input.

```
┌─ Book₀ ──────────────────────────────────────────
│ ΔFleetSeatAllocation
│ f?:        FLIGHT
│ s?:        SEAT
│ p?:        PERSON
├──────────────────────────────────────────────────
│ f? ∈ dom booked
│ f? hasSeat s?
│ s? ∉ dom (booked f?)
│ booked' = booked ⊕ {f? ↦ (booked f? ∪ {s? ↦ p?}) }
│ hasSeat' = hasSeat
└──────────────────────────────────────────────────
```

The flight must be known, the seat must be one that is assigned to this flight and the seat must not already be booked.

14.6.3 Cancelling a booking

An operation to cancel a booking needs to have flight, seat and person as input.

```
┌─ Cancel₀ ────────────────────────────────────────
│ ΔFleetSeatAllocation
│ f?:        FLIGHT
│ s?:        SEAT
│ p?:        PERSON
├──────────────────────────────────────────────────
│ f? ∈ dom booked
│ f? hasSeat s?
│ s? ↦ p? ∈ booked f?
│ booked' = booked ⊕ {f? ↦ (booked f? \ {s? ↦ p?}) }
│ hasSeat' = hasSeat
└──────────────────────────────────────────────────
```

The flight must be known, the seat must be assigned to this flight and the seat must be booked to the person.

14.7 Enquiry operations

14.7.1 Enquiry about a booking

An operation to enquire about a booking needs to have flight and seat as input:

REPLY ::= yes | no

```
┌─ Enquire ─────────────────────────────────────────────
│ ΞFleetSeatAllocation
│ f?:      FLIGHT
│ s?:      SEAT
│ taken!:  REPLY
│ who!:    PERSON
├────────────────────────────────────────────────────────
│ f? ∈ dom booked
│ f? hasSeat s?
│ ((s? ∈ dom booked f? ∧ taken! = yes ∧ who! = booked f? s?)
│ ∨
│ (s? ∉ dom booked f? ∧ taken! = no))
└────────────────────────────────────────────────────────
```

The flight must be known and the seat must be assigned to this flight.

14.8 Error conditions

This extended example has made preconditions of operations explicit. Error handling schemas can be defined to handle the violation of preconditions by returning a result value, as in previous examples. This part has been omitted here since it introduces no new ideas.

14.9 Conclusions

This more realistic specification is much more complex than the earlier examples and is nonetheless for a fairly modest system. It is wise to specify a simple version of any problem first, before taking on the entire complexity of any problem.

EXERCISES

A company lets its apartments to known customers for fixed time-slots. At any given time an apartment may only be booked to one person. A system is required to handle bookings. From time-to-time apartments are acquired and given up.

For a formal specification of this system give the following:

1. Schemas to describe the state of the system and an initialisation operation.

2. A schema for the operation to add a new customer.

3. A schema for the operation to acquire a new apartment.

4. A schema for the operation to make a booking of a given apartment to a given customer at a given time.

5. A schema for an enquiry operation to show all apartments which are free at a given time.

6. The Swiss Air Rescue organisation, REGA, has a fleet of helicopters that operate within Switzerland. Part of a formal specification for a control system for the helicopters is given here:

[AIRCRAFT] — the set of all aircraft
[POINT] — the set of all coordinates

$$
\begin{array}{ll}
\text{helis:} & \mathbb{P}\,\text{AIRCRAFT} \\
\text{Switzerland:} & \mathbb{P}\,\text{POINT} \\
\text{base:} & \text{AIRCRAFT} \nrightarrow \text{POINT} \\
\hline
\text{dom base} = \text{helis} \\
\text{ran base} \subseteq \text{Switzerland}
\end{array}
$$

The set *helis* is the set of aircraft (helicopters) operated by REGA. *Switzerland* is the set of points that are on Swiss territory. The function *base* gives the point that is the normal base for a given helicopter. Every REGA helicopter has a base and all REGA bases are in Switzerland.

The state of REGA's helicopters at any given time is given by the following: The functions *position, minsLeft* and *flightMins* respectively give the helicopter's current position, its remaining flying time in minutes and its flight time to a given point in minutes.

$$
\begin{array}{l}
\text{\_\_REGA} \\
\hline
\begin{array}{ll}
\text{position:} & \text{AIRCRAFT} \nrightarrow \text{POINT} \\
\text{minsLeft:} & \text{AIRCRAFT} \nrightarrow \mathbb{N} \\
\text{flightMins:} & \text{AIRCRAFT} \nrightarrow (\text{POINT} \nrightarrow \mathbb{N}) \\
\end{array} \\
\hline
\text{dom position} = \text{dom flightMins} = \text{dom minsLeft} = \text{helis}
\end{array}
$$

Use the variables from the schema *REGA* in answering the following questions.

(a) Explain the meaning of each component of the predicate of the schema *REGA*.
(b) Write an expression that states that all REGA's helicopters are currently within Switzerland.
(c) Write an expression to state that any point in Switzerland can be reached by a REGA helicopter within 15 minutes.
(d) Write an expression to state that each REGA helicopter is currently at a REGA base.
(e) Write an expression to state that each REGA helicopter is currently at its own base.
(f) Write a expression to state that every REGA helicopter has enough flying time left to reach a REGA base.

Hints on creating specifications

15.1 Introduction

The process of creating formal specifications needs more than fluency with the mathematical tools provided by the Z notation. It requires imagination and investigation and the ability to revise one's work when difficulties arise and when a new approach offers itself. It has been said that the most important aid to formal specification is a large waste-paper basket!

This chapter offers some hints on how to go about creating formal specifications.

15.2 Types

Find out what the sets (types) in the system to be specified are. Keep these sets general. The style which uses 'the set of all …' allows you to consider a subset and to add new elements from the 'set of all' to the subset and to remove elements from the subset.

For example, if you declare

[STUDENT]   the set of students at this university

you cannot enrol any new students or allow students to leave, since the type is fixed.

The following is far better:

[PERSON]   the set of all persons

students: $\mathbb{P}$PERSON

Be sure that your types are truly *atomic*. For example, don't declare a type *CLASS* meaning a *group of* students. Instead, use the type *PERSON* as above and make *class* a subset.

15.3 Relationships

Next consider the relationships between the types. By discovering how many values of what type are related to how many of the other type, find out if any of the *relations* are *functions*. If so, are the functions *total* or *partial*, or *injective*? Are there any relationships between the relations and functions you have found? For example, must they have the same domains or must the domain of one contain the range of another?

If there is a natural order to some values, then think of using a sequence; otherwise it is easier to work with sets.

Remember that it is necessary to state the obvious!

15.4 The state

This investigation of relationships will lead to a schema which represents the *state*. You will also have discovered some *invariants*, which are included in the state schema.

15.5 Initialisation operation

You will need to provide an initialisation operation that sets up an initial state. This *initial* state should be as simple as possible. Often it gives empty sets and relationships as the starting point. It is important that the initial state should not violate any invariant of the system. Ideally, this will be *formally proved*. With a simple initial state it is usually easy to see that the invariants are not violated.

15.6 Operations

Start by considering the behaviour of each operation only when it is given sensible values. Include a check that the values are reasonable (the *precondition*), but do not deal with errors at this stage. At a later stage define a separate schema to deal with errors by returning a reply value.

Don't forget to state explicitly what does *not* change as a result of an operation.

15.7 Enquiry operations

Enquiry operations do not *change* the state, and thus cannot violate an invariant. Use a *xi* (Ξ) schema where possible.

15.8   In case of severe difficulty

If the specification is getting too hard, try viewing it in a more *abstract* way. Hide some of the details for now and try to take a broader view. Put the detail back in later when you have a better understanding of what you are trying to do.

Example specifications

16.1   The Airport example

The air-traffic control of an airport keeps a record of the *planes waiting* to land and the *assignment* of planes to *gates* on the ground. There are operations to accept a plane when it *arrives* in the airport's waiting space, to *assign* a plane to a gate at the airport and to record that a plane *leaves* its gate.

16.2   The types

The types used in this formal specification are:

[PLANE]	the set of all possible, uniquely identified planes
[GATE]	the set of all gates at this airport

16.3   The state

The state of the *airport*, at any time, can be expressed by this Z *schema*:

AIRPORT_____

waiting: $\mathbb{P}$ PLANE
assignment: GATE $\rightarrowtail$ PLANE

――――――――――――――――

waiting ∩ ran assignment = ∅

Each plane is assigned to at most one gate and each gate has at most one plane assigned to it; so the assignment of planes to gates is an *injective* (one-to-one) *function* from gate to plane.

Figure 16.1

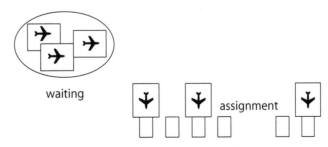

waiting   assignment

The planes waiting are a *set* of planes (they are in no particular order). No plane is both waiting and assigned to a gate.

16.4 The initialisation operation

Initially there are no planes waiting or at any gate.

```
┌─ Init ──────────────────────
│ AIRPORT'
├─────────────────────────────
│ waiting' = ∅
│ assignment' = ∅
└─────────────────────────────
```

The schema has access to the variables of the schema *AIRPORT*. The set *waiting* is the *empty* set. The function *assignment* is an *empty* function.

16.5 The operations

16.5.1 Arrive

The operation *Arrive* records the arrival of a plane *p?* in the airport's waiting area:

```
┌─ Arrive ────────────────────────────
│ p?:      PLANE
│ ΔAIRPORT
├─────────────────────────────────────
│ p? ∉ (waiting ∪ ran assignment)
│ waiting' = waiting ∪ {p?}
│ assignment' = assignment
└─────────────────────────────────────
```

The plane must be neither already waiting nor assigned to a gate. The schema has access to the before and after (') values of the schema *AIRPORT*. The new value of the set *waiting* is the same as before but with *p?* added. The new value of the function *assignment* is the same as the old value of *assignment*.

16.5.2 Assign

The operation *Assign* records the assignment of a plane *p?* to a free gate *g?*:

```
  Assign_____

    p?:       PLANE
    g?:       GATE
    ΔAIRPORT
  _____

    p? ∈ waiting
    g? ∉ dom assignment
    assignment' = assignment ∪ {g? ↦ p?}
    waiting' = waiting \ {p?}
```

The plane must be waiting and the gate must be free. The pairing between gate *g?* and plane *p?* is added to *assignment*. Plane *p?* is removed from *waiting*.

16.5.3   Leave

The operation *Leave* records the plane *p?* leaving its gate:

```
  Leave_____

    p?:       PLANE
    ΔAIRPORT
  _____

    p? ∈ ran assignment
    assignment' = assignment ▷ {p?}
    waiting' = waiting
```

The plane *p?* must be assigned to a gate. The assignment for plane *p?* is removed. The waiting planes are unaffected.

16.6   Handling errors

So far we have indicated the preconditions for successful operations, but have not said what will happen if these preconditions are not satisfied. We can do this by using separate error-handling schemas.

Firstly we introduce a type for a result message:

RESULT ::= OK | full | badAircraft | notWaiting | gateNotFree | notAtGate

16.7   Error-handling operations

We introduce a further, output (!), parameter, *reply!*, to each error schema; the Ξ in the schema name Ξ*AIRPORT* signifies that there will be no change to the state of the airport.

131

16.7.1   ArriveErr

This schema handles the cases where the preconditions of *Arrive* are not satisfied:

```
┌─ ArriveErr ──────────────────────────────────────────
│ p?:            PLANE
│ reply!:        RESULT
│ ΞAIRPORT
├──────────────────────────────────────────────────────
│ #waiting  = limit ∧ reply! = full
│ ∨
│ p? ∈ (waiting ∪ ran assignment) ∧ reply! = badAircraft
└──────────────────────────────────────────────────────
```

16.7.2   AssignErr

The operation *AssignErr* handles the cases where the preconditions of *Assign* are not satisfied:

```
┌─ AssignErr ──────────────────────────────────────────
│ p?:            PLANE
│ g?:            GATE
│ reply!:        RESULT
│ ΞAIRPORT
├──────────────────────────────────────────────────────
│ p? ∉ waiting ∧ reply! = notWaiting
│ ∨
│ g? ∈ dom assignment ∧ reply! = gateNotFree
└──────────────────────────────────────────────────────
```

16.7.3   LeaveErr

The operation *LeaveErr* handles the cases where the preconditions of *Leave* are not satisfied:

```
┌─ LeaveErr ───────────────────────────────────────────
│ p?: PLANE
│ reply!: RESULT
│ ΞAIRPORT
├──────────────────────────────────────────────────────
│ p? ∉ ran assignment ∧ reply! = notAtGate
└──────────────────────────────────────────────────────
```

16.8 Fully specified operations

Finally, we use *schema calculus* to put together the schemas to give fully specified operations.

We start with a small schema *OKMessage* that simply produces the reply *OK*:

OKMessage == [reply!: RESULT | reply! = OK]

Then we combine schemas using schema operators.

16.9 The operations

16.9.1 Arrive

The operation *Arrive* records the arrival of a plane *p?* in the airport's waiting area:

Arrive == $Arrive_0 \wedge$ OKMessage $\vee$ ArriveErr

The *Arrive* operation behaves either like the $Arrive_0$ operation conjoined with the *OKMessage* operation, or like the *ArriveErr* operation.

16.9.2 Assign

The operation *Assign* records the assignment of a plane *p?* to a free gate *g?*:

Assign == $Assign_0 \wedge$ OKMessage $\vee$ AssignErr

The *Assign* operation behaves either like the $Assign_0$ operation conjoined with the *OKMessage* operation, or like the *AssignErr* operation.

16.9.3 $Leave_0$

The operation *Leave* records the plane *p?* leaving its gate:

Leave == $Leave_0 \wedge$ OKMessage $\vee$ LeaveErr

The *Leave* operation behaves either like the $Leave_0$ operation conjoined with the *OKMessage* operation, or like the *LeaveErr* operation.

16.10 The Library example

A library has a stock of books which may be taken out by its registered members.

16.11 Types

[BOOK]   the set of all possible uniquely identified books
[PERSON]   the set of all possible persons

16.12 State

```
┌─ LIB₀ ──────────────────────────────
│ stock:      ℙBOOK
│ members:    ℙPERSON
│ outTo:      BOOK ⇸ PERSON
├─────────────────────────────────────
│ dom outTo ⊆ stock
│ ran outTo ⊆ members
└─────────────────────────────────────
```

Only books which are in the library's *stock* can be recorded as *out to* a *member*. Only registered members may take out books.

16.13 Initialisation operation

Initially the library has no stock of books and no members and no books are recorded as out to members.

```
┌─ Init₀ ─────────────────────────────
│ LIB₀'
├─────────────────────────────────────
│ stock' = ∅
│ members' = ∅
│ outTo' = ∅
└─────────────────────────────────────
```

16.14 Operations

16.14.1 Acquire book

The book must not already belong to the library's stock. It is added to the stock. The members remain unchanged.

```
  ┌─ Acquire₀ ─────────────────
  │ ΔLIB₀
  │ b?:        BOOK
  ├────────────────────────────
  │ b? ∉ stock
  │ stock' = stock ∪ {b?}
  │ members' = members
  │ outTo' = outTo
  └────────────────────────────
```

16.14.2   Register member

The person must not already be a member. The person becomes a member. The stock remains unchanged.

```
  ┌─ Register₀ ─────────────────────
  │ ΔLIB₀
  │ p?:        PERSON
  ├──────────────────────────────────
  │ p? ∉ members
  │ members' = members ∪ {p?}
  │ stock' = stock
  │ outTo' = outTo
  └──────────────────────────────────
```

16.14.3   Take a book out

The person must be a member. The book must be part of the library's stock and must not be out to anyone. The book becomes recorded as out to the member. The members and stock are unchanged.

```
  ┌─ TakeOut₀ ─────────────────────
  │ ΔLIB₀
  │ p?:        PERSON
  │ b?:        BOOK
  ├──────────────────────────────────
  │ p? ∈ members
  │ b? ∈ stock \ dom outTo
  │ outTo' = outTo ∪ {b? ↦ p?}
  │ member' = member
  │ stock' = stock
  └──────────────────────────────────
```

16.14.4 Bring back

The book must be recorded as out. The reference to the book being out is removed. The members and stock are unchanged.

```
┌─ BringBack₀ ──────────────────
│ ΔLIB₀
│ b?:        BOOK
├───────────────────────────────
│ b? ∈ dom outTo
│ outTo' = {b?} ◁ outTo
│ member' = member
│ stock' = stock
└───────────────────────────────
```

16.14.5 Dispose of a book

The book must belong to the library and not be out to a member. The book is removed from the stock. The members and the record of what books are out are unchanged.

```
┌─ Dispose₀ ────────────────────
│ ΔLIB₀
│ b?:        BOOK
├───────────────────────────────
│ b? ∈ stock \ dom outTo
│ stock' = stock \ {b?}
│ members' = members
│ outTo' = outTo
└───────────────────────────────
```

16.14.6 De-register member

The person must be a member who has no books out. The person is removed from the membership. The stock and record of books out are unchanged.

```
┌─ Deregister₀ ─────────────────
│ ΔLIB₀
│ p?:        PERSON
├───────────────────────────────
│ p? ∈ members \ ran outTo
│ members' = members \ {p?}
│ stock' = stock
│ outTo' = outTo
└───────────────────────────────
```

16.15   Extension 1: Limit on number of books out

There is a *limit* to the number of books a member may take out.

limit: $\mathbb{N}$

---

limit $\in$ 1..10

The limit lies between 1 and 10. It will be the same for all members.

16.16   The state

The state is modified to reflect the fact that no member may ever have taken out more books than the limit.

LIB_1 _____

LIB_0

$\forall p: PERSON \mid p \in members \bullet$
$\#(outTo \rhd \{p\}) \leq limit$

For each person *p* who is a member, the size of the *outTo* relation range restricted to the set containing just the person *p* (the number of books that are out to person *p*) must not exceed the limit.

The schema LIB_1 can be expanded to:

LIB_1 _____

stock:	$\mathbb{P}BOOK$
members:	$\mathbb{P}PERSON$
outTo:	$BOOK \nrightarrow PERSON$

---

dom outTo $\subseteq$ stock
ran outTo $\subseteq$ members
$\forall p: PERSON \mid p \in members \bullet$
  $\#(outTo \rhd \{p\}) \leq limit$

16.17   Initialisation operation

The new initialisation operation is identical to the previous one, except that it applies to the extended state schema.

$Init_1 == Init_0 [LIB_1{}'/LIB_0{}']$

The initial state satisfies the new state invariant.
The schema $Init_1$ can be expanded to:

```
┌─ Init₁ ─────────────────────────
│ LIB₁'
│────────────────────────────────
│ stock' = ∅
│ members' = ∅
│ outTo' = ∅
```

16.18 Operations

The operations of acquiring a book, registering a member, disposing of a book, de-registering a member and bringing back a book, are all unaffected by the new requirement:

$$Acquire_1 == Acquire_0 \; [\Delta LIB_1 / \Delta LIB_0]$$

$$Register_1 == Register_0 \; [\Delta LIB_1 / \Delta LIB0]$$

$$Dispose_1 == Dispose_0 \; [\Delta LIB_1 / \Delta LIB_0]$$

$$Deregister_1 == Deregister_0 \; [\Delta LIB_1 / \Delta LIB_0]$$

$$BringBack_1 == BringBack_0 \; [\Delta LIB_1 / \Delta LIB_0]$$

These new operations are identical to the previous ones, except that they apply to the new state schema.

16.18.1 Taking a book out

When a member attempts to take a book out, there is a check that the limit would not be exceeded.

```
┌─ TakeOut₁ ─────────────────────
│ TakeOut₀ [ΔLIB₁/ΔLIB₀]
│────────────────────────────────
│ #(outTo ▷ {p?}) < limit
```

For the person $p?$ the size of the $outTo$ relation range restricted to the set containing just the person $p?$ (the number of books that are out to person $p?$) must not yet have reached the limit.

16.19 Extension 2: Books out for a limited period

We now consider a library where the books may be borrowed for limited number of days. There is no charge for taking out books, but a fine is payable for late return.

16.20 Types

We introduce the type *dates*. We will represent *money* as whole numbers of currency units, possibly negative:

[DATE]   the set of all possible dates

MONEY == $\mathbb{Z}$

All members may take out books for the same *period* of days.

$$period: \mathbb{N}$$

Books returned late incur the same *fine* each day.

$$
\begin{array}{|l}
fine: MONEY \\
\hline
fine \geq 0
\end{array}
$$

16.21 The state

The *date* that each book was taken *out* is recorded. The amount that each member owes (even if nothing) is recorded.

$$
\begin{array}{|l}
\underline{LIB_2} \\
\begin{array}{|l}
LIB_1 \\
dateOut:\quad BOOK \rightarrowtail DATE \\
owes:\qquad PERSON \rightarrowtail MONEY \\
\hline
dom\ dateOut = dom\ outTo \\
dom\ owes = member
\end{array}
\end{array}
$$

16.22 Initialisation operation

The initial state is extended to show that there is no information recorded about dates that books were taken out or about money owing:

$$
\begin{array}{|l}
\hline
\text{Init}_2 \\\\
\hline
\text{Init}_1 \ [\text{LIB}_2/\text{LIB}_1] \\\\
\hline
\text{dateOut}' = \varnothing \\
\text{owes}' = \varnothing \\
\hline
\end{array}
$$

16.23   Operations

The operations to acquire a book and to dispose of a book are unchanged.

$$\text{Acquire}_2 == \text{Acquire}_1 \ [\Delta\text{LIB}_2/\Delta\text{LIB}_1]$$

$$\text{Dispose}_2 == \text{Dispose}_1 \ [\Delta\text{LIB}_2/\Delta\text{LIB}_1]$$

16.23.1   Register member

A new member owes nothing.

$$
\begin{array}{|l}
\hline
\text{Register}_2 \\\\
\hline
\text{Register}_1 \ [\Delta\text{LIB}_2/\Delta\text{LIB}_1] \\\\
\hline
\text{owes}' = \text{owes} \cup \{p? \mapsto 0\} \\
\text{dateOut}' = \text{dateOut} \\
\hline
\end{array}
$$

16.23.2   De-register member

To be de-registered the member must not owe anything or be in credit.

$$
\begin{array}{|l}
\hline
\text{Deregister}_2 \\\\
\hline
\text{Deregister}_1 \ [\Delta\text{LIB}_2/\Delta\text{LIB}_1] \\\\
\hline
\text{owes} \ p? = 0 \\
\text{dateOut}' = \text{dateOut} \\
\hline
\end{array}
$$

16.23.3   Taking a book out

The date that the book is taken out is recorded.

```
  ┌─ TakeOut₂ ──────────────────────────────
  │ TakeOut₁ [ΔLIB₂/ΔLIB₁]
  │ d?:        DATE
  │ ─────────────────────────────────────────
  │ dateOut' = dateOut ∪ {b? ↦ d?}
  │ owes' = owes
  │
  └──────────────────────────────────────────
```

16.23.4 Bring back

We specify that there should be a function $Diff(d1, d2)$ that returns the number of working days that $d2$ is later than $d1$:

$$Diff: DATE \times DATE \rightarrow \mathbb{Z}$$

If the book is returned within the period then there is no change in what the member owes. If the book is late then the member's debt is increased by a fixed fine for each day late. This is calcutaed only when the book is brought back:

```
  ┌─ BringBack₂ ─────────────────────────────
  │ BringBack₁ [ΔLIB₂/ΔLIB₁]
  │ today?:   DATE
  │ ─────────────────────────────────────────
  │ dateOut' = {b?} ⊲ dateOut ∧
  │ ( Diff ((dateOut b?) today?) ≤ period ∧
  │   owes' = owes)
  │     ∨
  │ (Diff ((dateOut b?) today?) > period ∧
  │   owes' = owes ⊕
  │   {outTo b? ↦ owes outTo b? +
  │     (Diff ((dateOut b?) today?) − period) * fine})
  │
  └──────────────────────────────────────────
```

The date that the book was taken out is removed from the *dateOut* function.

If the difference between the date when the book was taken out and today's date is within the period, then the amount the person owes stays the same.

If the difference between the date the book was taken out and today's date exceeds the period, then the amount owed by the person who took the book out is increased by the fine amount for each day over the period.

16.23.5 PayIn

A member may *pay in* an *amount* of money (positive) to offset current or future money owed. Everything else remains unchanged.

$\begin{array}{|l}
\hline
\text{PayIn}_2 \\
\hline
\Delta\text{LIB}_2 \\
\Xi\text{LIB}_1 \\
\text{p?:} \qquad \text{PERSON} \\
\text{amount?: MONEY} \\
\hline
\text{p?} \in \text{members} \\
\text{amount?} > 0 \\
\text{owes'} = \text{owes} \cup \{\text{p?} \mapsto \text{owes p?} - \text{amount?}\} \\
\text{dateOut'} = \text{dateOut} \\
\hline
\end{array}$

16.24 Extension 3: Reservations

We now extend the library system to allow members to reserve titles.

16.25 Types

A member will wish to reserve a *title*, rather than a particular *book*.

[TITLE]   the set of all possible book titles

16.26 The state

The *title* is known of every book in stock. *Reservations* are allowed for every title for which there is a book in stock. Only members may reserve *titles* and they can only reserve each title once. A book which belongs to the library and which is not out may be *held for* a member (who has previously reserved it and will later collect it).

$\begin{array}{|l}
\hline
\text{LIB}_3 \\
\hline
\text{LIB}_3 \\
\text{title:} \qquad \text{BOOK} \rightarrowtail \text{TITLE} \\
\text{reserved: TITLE} \nrightarrow \text{iseq PERSON} \\
\text{heldFor: BOOK} \nrightarrow \text{PERSON} \\
\hline
\text{dom title} = \text{stock} \\
\text{dom reserved} = \text{ran title} \\
(\forall \text{t: TITLE} \mid \text{t} \in \text{dom reserved} \bullet \\
\quad \text{ran (reserved t)} \subseteq \text{members}) \\
\text{dom heldFor} \subseteq \text{stock} \setminus \text{dom outTo} \\
\text{ran heldFor} \subseteq \text{members} \\
\hline
\end{array}$

16.27   Initialisation operation

Initially there are no titles recorded, no titles reserved and no books held for members.

```
┌─ Init₃ ──────────────────────────
│ Init₂ [LIB₃'/LIB₂']
│ ─────────────────────────────────
│ title' = ∅
│ reserved' = ∅
│ heldFor' = ∅
└───────────────────────────────────
```

16.28   Operations

16.28.1   Acquire a book

The title of a book is recorded when it is acquired. If the title is new then an empty reservation list is set up for it, otherwise reservations are unchanged. Books held are unchanged.

```
┌─ Acquire₃ ───────────────────────
│ Acquire₂ [ΔLIB₃/ΔLIB₂]
│ t?:         TITLE
│ ─────────────────────────────────
│ title' = title ∪ {b? ↦ t?}
│ (t? ∉ dom reserved ∧
│   reserved' = reserved ∪
│ {t? ↦ ⟨ ⟩})
│ ∨
│ (t? ∈ dom reserved ∧
│   reserved' = reserved)
│ heldFor' = heldFor
└───────────────────────────────────
```

16.28.2   Reserve a title

The person reserving must be a member and must not already have reserved this title. The library must have a book of this title in stock.

$Reserve_3$
_____

ΔLIB_3
ΞLIB_2
p?:   PERSON
t?:   TITLE

---

p? $\in$ members
p? $\notin$ ran (reserved t?)
t? $\in$ ran title
reserved' = reserved $\oplus$
  {t? $\mapsto$ reserved t? $^\frown$ $\langle$p?$\rangle$}
title' = title
heldFor' = heldFor

Collected notation

A.1 General

[X]   the basic type X

data type ::= member$_1$ | member$_2$ | ... | member$_n$

X == Y   abbreviation definition – X stands for Y

A.2 Sets

$\mathbb{Z}$	the type integer (whole numbers)
$\mathbb{N}$	the set of natural numbers (≥ 0)
$\mathbb{N}_1$	the set of positive natural numbers (≥ 1)
$t \in S$	t is an element of S
$t \notin S$	t is not an element of S
$S \subseteq T$	S is contained in T.
$\emptyset$ or { }	the empty set
$\{t_1, t_2, \dots t_n\}$	the set containing $t_1, t_2, \dots t_n$
$\mathbb{P}S$	Powerset: the set of all subsets of S
$S \cup T$	Union: elements that are either in S or T
$S \cap T$	Intersection: elements that are both in S and in T
$S \setminus T$	Difference: elements that are in S but not in T
#S	Size: the number of elements in S
$\bigcup$ SS	the distributed union of the set of sets SS
$\bigcap$ SS	the distributed intersection of the set of sets SS
disjoint sqs	the sets in the sequence sqs are disjoint
sqs partition S	the sets in sqs partition the set S

A.3 Logic

true, false	logical constants
$\neg P$	negation: 'not P'
$P \wedge Q$	conjunction: 'P and Q'
$P \vee Q$	disjunction: 'P or Q'
$P \Rightarrow Q$	implication: 'P implies Q' or 'if P then Q'

$$P \Leftrightarrow Q \qquad \text{equivalence: 'P is logically equivalent to Q'}$$
$$t_1 = t_2 \qquad \text{equality between terms}$$
$$t_1 \neq t_2 \qquad \neg(t_1 = t_2)$$

A.4 Schemas

```
__SchemaName_____
  declarations
_____
  predicate
_____
```

SchemaName == [declarations | predicate]

A.4.1 Axiomatic definition

```
|  declarations
|_____
|  predicate
```

A.4.2 Inclusion

```
__IncludeS_____
  c:          ℕ
  S
_____
  c < 10
_____
```

==

```
__IncludeS_____
  c:          ℕ
  a, b:       ℕ
_____
  c < 10
  a < b
_____
```

A.4.3 Conjunction

```
__T_____
  b, c:       ℕ
_____
  b < c
_____
```

146

$SandT == S \wedge T$

```
__SandT_____
|
|  a, b, c:   ℕ
|_____
|
|  a < b
|  b < c
|_____
```

A.4.4   Disjunction

```
__SorT_____
|
|  a, b, c:   ℕ
|_____
|
|  a < b ∨ b < c
|_____
```

$SorT == S \vee T$

A.4.5   Decoration

```
__S'_____
|
|  a', b':   ℕ
|_____
|
|  a' < b'
|_____
```

A.5   Predicates and their use with schemas

$\forall x : T \bullet P$	Universal quantification: 'for all x of type T, P holds'
$\exists x : T \bullet P$	Existential quantification: 'there exists an x of type T, where P holds'
$\exists_1 x : T \bullet P$	Unique existence: 'there exists a unique x of type T, such that P holds'
$\{D \mid P \bullet t\}$	the set of t's where given declarations D, P holds
$S[new / old, \ldots]$	schema renaming
$S \setminus (x_1, x_2, \ldots x_n)$	schema hiding
$S \upharpoonright (x_1, x_2, \ldots x_n)$	schema projection
$S \mathbin{;} T$	schema composition: S, then T

A.6 Relations

$X \times Y$	the set of ordered pairs of X's and Y's
$X \leftrightarrow Y$	the set of relations from X to Y: $== \mathbb{P}(X \times Y)$
$x \, R \, y$	x is related by R to y: $== (x, y) \in R$
$x \mapsto y$	$== (x, y)$
$\{ x_1 \mapsto y_1, x_2 \mapsto y_2, \ldots, x_n \mapsto y_n \}$	
	$==$ the relation $\{ (x_1, y_1), (x_2, y_2), \ldots, (x_n, y_n) \}$ relating x_1 to y_1, x_2 to y_2, $\ldots$, x_n to y_n
$\text{dom} \, R$	the domain of a relation
	$== \{x: X \mid (\exists y: Y \bullet x \, R \, y) \bullet x\}$
$\text{ran} \, R$	the range of a relation
	$== \{y: Y \mid (\exists x: X \bullet x \, R \, y) \bullet y\}$
$R(S)$	the relational image of S in R
$S \lhd R$	the relation R domain restricted to S
$R \rhd S$	the relation R range restricted to S
$S \ntriangleleft R$	the relation R domain anti-restricted to S
$R \ntriangleright S$	the relation R range anti-restricted to S
$R \, ; \, Q$	the forward composition of R with Q
$Q \circ R$	the backward composition of Q with R
R^{+}	the repeated self-composition of R
R^{*}	the repeated self-composition of R
	$== R^{+} \cup \text{id} \, X$
$\text{id} \, X$	$\{x: X \bullet x \mapsto x\}$
$R^{\sim}$	the inverse of R

A.7 Functions

$X \nrightarrow Y$	the set of partial functions from X to Y:
	$== \{f: X \leftrightarrow Y \mid (\forall x: X \mid x \in \text{dom} \, f \bullet (\exists_1 y: Y \bullet x \, f \, y)) \bullet f\}$
$X \rightarrow Y$	the set of total functions from X to Y:
	$== \{f: X \nrightarrow Y \mid \text{dom} \, f = X \bullet f\}$
$X \nrightarrowtail Y$	the set of partial injective functions from X to Y:
	$== \{f: X \nrightarrow Y \mid f^{\sim} \in Y \nrightarrow X \bullet f\}$
$X \rightarrowtail Y$	the set of total injective functions from X to Y:
	$== \{f: X \nrightarrowtail Y \mid \text{dom} \, f = X \bullet f\}$
$X \nrightarrow\!\!\!\rightarrow Y$	the partial surjective functions from X to Y:
	$== \{f: X \nrightarrow Y \mid \text{ran} \, f = Y\}$
$X \rightarrow\!\!\!\rightarrow Y$	the total surjective functions from X to Y:
	$== \{f: X \nrightarrow\!\!\!\rightarrow Y \mid \text{dom} \, f = X\}$
$X \rightarrowtail\!\!\!\rightarrow Y$	the bijective functions from X to Y (total, injective and surjective)
	$== (X \rightarrow Y) \cap (X \rightarrowtail Y)$

f x *or* f(x)   the function f applied to x

f ⊕ g   functional overriding == (dom g ⊲ f) ∪ g

A.8   Sequences

seq X   the set of sequences whose elements are drawn from X

                                     == {S: $\mathbb{N} \nrightarrow X$ | dom S = 1 .. #S}

seq_1 X   set of non-empty sequences

iseq X   set of injective sequences (no duplicates)

#S   the length of the sequence S

⟨ ⟩   the empty sequence { }

⟨ x_1, ... x_n ⟩   == { 1 ↦ x_1, ..., n ↦ x_n}

⟨ x_1, ... x_n ⟩ ⌢ ⟨ y_1, ... y_n ⟩   concatenation:

                                     == ⟨ x_1, ... x_n , y_1, ... y_n ⟩

head S   == S 1

last S   == S #S

tail (⟨ x ⟩ ⌢ S)   == S

front (S ⌢ ⟨ x ⟩)   == S

squash f   the function f (f: $\mathbb{N} \nrightarrow X$) squashed into a sequence

S ↾ s   the sequence S filtered to elements in s

                                     == squash (S ▷ s)

rev S   the sequence S in reverse order

Solutions to exercises

Chapter 1

1.
(a) Monday – clearly the Friday is the 27th.
(b) Sunday – the whole weekend, so Friday = 28th.
(c) Saturday – is the weekend beginning 29th in September or not? It starts in September but ends on 1st October. Perhaps the event starts on the 22nd?
(d) Friday – is Friday part of a weekend? Does the event start on the 30th or on the 23rd?

A better specification would be, for example: 'The event takes place on the weekend which includes the last Sunday in September'.

2.
▶ **First ambiguity:** What does 'next' Wednesday mean, when you are reading on a Monday – Wednesday 6th or Wednesday of next week, the 13th?
▶ **Second ambiguity:** Does on leave until Wednesday mean that the software engineer's last day of leave is Wednesday, or does it mean that the software engineer will be back on Wednesday?

The colleague might reasonably expect the software engineer next to be back at work on any of: Wednesday 6th, Thursday 7th, Wednesday 13th or Thursday 14th.

3. Some of these questions are answered by user handbooks. Several are not. Answers from a particular user manual:
(a) Invalid dates such as 31st April, day number not accepted.
(b) 29th February – question not dealt with by handbook, but since recorder does not

store year it cannot know if 29th February exists or not.
(c) Overlapping requests – not dealt with by handbook.
(d) New Year's Eve – not mentioned, but no problem.
(e) Ordering of requests – not mentioned, but order does not matter.

4. You can't tell, but it matters a lot, because this is genuinely ambiguous. (This was a real specification!)

5. Manuals tend to be unclear; the user may need to experiment to find out what will happen.

Chapter 2

1.
[PERSON] the set of all uniquely identifiable persons
users, loggedIn: $\mathbb{P}$ PERSON
loggedIn $\subseteq$ users

2.
>limit: $\mathbb{N}$
>\# loggedIn $\leq$ limit

3. Add:
>staff, customers: $\mathbb{P}$ PERSON

and
>staff $\cap$ customers = $\varnothing$
>staff $\cup$ customers = users

or
>⟨staff, customers⟩ partition users

4.
>loggedIn $\subseteq$ staff
>\#customer > \#staff

5.

(a) compulsories ⊆ acceptables

(b) #compulsories = 3

(c) firstAcc ≠ secondAcc

(d) firstAcc ∩ secondAcc ≠ ∅

Chapter 3

1. Invariant property. Only registered users can ever be logged-in.

> loggedIn ⊆ users

2. Initialisation operation: no users, no-one logged in. This satisfies the invariant.

> users' = ∅
> loggedIn' = ∅

3. Add new user. Person p must not already be a user. Person p is added to *users*.

> p: PERSON
>
> p ∉ users
> users' = users ∪ {p}
> loggedIn' = loggedIn

4. Remove user. Person p must already be a user. Person p is removed from *users*.

> p: PERSON
>
> p ∈ users
> p ∉ loggedIn
> users' = users \ {p}
> loggedIn' = loggedIn

5.

(a) Log in:

> p ∈ users
> p ∉ loggedIn
> loggedIn' = loggedIn ∪ {p}
> users' = users

(b) Log out:

> p ∈ users
> p ∈ loggedIn
> loggedIn' = loggedIn \ {p}
> users' = users

Chapter 4

1. Law about implication

P	Q	P ⇒ Q
false	false	true
false	true	true
true	false	false
true	true	true

P	Q	¬P	¬P ∨ Q	P ⇒ Q ⇔ ¬P ∨ Q
false	false	true	true	true
false	true	true	true	true
true	false	false	false	true
true	true	false	true	true

2.

P	Q	P ⇒ Q	Q ⇒ P
false	false	true	true
false	true	true	false
true	false	false	true
true	true	true	true

P ⇒ Q ∧ Q ⇒ P	P ⇔ Q
true	true
false	false
false	false
true	true

3.

> ¬(p ∉ onboard ∧ #onboard < capacity)
> ⇔
> ¬(p ∉ onboard) ∨ ¬(#onboard < capacity)
> ⇔
> p ∈ onboard ∨ #onboard ≥ capacity

4.

> (a ∧ b) ∨ (a ∧ c) ∨ (a ∧ ¬c)
> ⇔ a ∧ (b ∨ c ∨ ¬c)
> ⇔ a ∧ (b ∨ true)
> ⇔ a ∧ true
> ⇔ a

5. The only way in which

> p ∈ loggedIn ∧ p ∈ user

can be true is if both

> p ∈ loggedIn

and

> p ∈ user

are true. But, because of the given implication, if

> p ∈ loggedIn

is true, then so is

> p ∈ user

6.

$x \neq 2 \vee x \neq 6$ is

$\neg(x = 2 \wedge x = 6)$ is

$\neg$false istrue;

any number is either different from 2 or different from 6

7.

$s = t \wedge s \neq EOF$

if s is the same as t, and s is different from EOF, then t must be different from EOF.

8.

$x \leq y$

9.

$x = 0$

10.

$age < 16 \wedge \neg student$

Chapter 5

1.

RESPONSE ::=
OK | AlreadyAUser | NotAUser | LoggedIn | NotLoggedIn

2. Add new user:

p: PERSON
reply: RESPONSE

loggedIn' = loggedIn

$\wedge$

$((p \notin users \wedge$
$users' = users \cup \{p\} \wedge$
$reply = OK)$

$\vee$

$(p \in users \wedge$
$users' = users \wedge$
$reply = AlreadyAUser))$

3. Remove user. This answer makes use of the invariant of this system:

loggedIn $\subseteq$ users

which implies that

$p \notin users \Rightarrow p \notin loggedIn$
p: PERSON
reply: RESPONSE

loggedIn' = loggedIn

$\wedge$

$((p \in users \wedge p \notin loggedIn \wedge$
$users' = users \setminus \{p\} \wedge reply = OK)$

$\vee$

$(p \notin users \wedge$
$users' = users \wedge reply = NotAUser)$

$\vee$

$(p \in users \wedge p \in loggedIn \wedge$
$users' = users \wedge reply = LoggedIn))$

4. Log in:

p: PERSON
reply: RESPONSE

users' = users

$\wedge$

$((p \in users \wedge p \notin loggedIn \wedge$
$loggedIn' = loggedIn \cup \{p\} \wedge reply = OK)$

$\vee$

$(p \notin users \wedge$
$loggedIn' = loggedIn \wedge reply = NotAUser)$

$\vee$

$(p \in loggedIn \wedge$
$loggedIn' = loggedIn \wedge reply = LoggedIn))$

5. Log out:

p: PERSON
reply: RESPONSE

users' = users

$\wedge$

$((p \in loggedIn \wedge$
$loggedIn' = loggedIn \setminus \{p\} \wedge reply = OK)$

$\vee$

$(p \notin users \wedge$
$loggedIn' = loggedIn \wedge reply = NotAUser)$

$\vee$

$(p \in users \wedge p \notin loggedIn \wedge$
$loggedIn' = loggedIn \wedge reply = NotLoggedIn))$

Chapter 6

1. *LinesRemaining*

LinesRemaining_____

ΞCursor
lines!: $\mathbb{N}$

---

lines! = numLines − line

---

or

```
┌─ LinesRemaining ──────────────
│ ΔCursor
│ lines!:    ℕ
├───────────────────────────────
│ lines! = numLines – line
│ line' = line
│ column' = column
└───────────────────────────────
```

2.   *UpKey*. This schema deals with what happens when the cursor is not on the top line of the display:

```
┌─ UpKeyNormal ─────────────────
│ ΔCursor
│ key?:    KEY
├───────────────────────────────
│ key? = up
│ line > 1
│ line' = line – 1
│ column' = column
└───────────────────────────────
```

The next schema deals with what happens when the cursor is on the top line of the display:

```
┌─ UpKeyAtTop ──────────────────
│ ΔCursor
│ key?:    KEY
├───────────────────────────────
│ key? = up
│ line = 1
│ line' = line – 1
│ line' = numLines
└───────────────────────────────
```

Note that the cursor has been defined to *wrap round* to the bottom line of the display. The full behaviour is given by:

$$\text{UpKey} == \text{UpKeyNormal} \lor \text{UpKeyAtTop}$$

3.   *LeftKey*. The operation for moving left is given. It is easiest to deal first with what happens when the cursor is not at the far left of the display:

```
┌─ LeftKeyNormal ───────────────
│ ΔCursor
│ key?:    KEY
├───────────────────────────────
│ key? = left
│ column > 1
│ column' = column – 1
│ line' = line
└───────────────────────────────
```

The next schema deals with the cursor's being at the left of a line other than the top line of the display. Note that the cursor wraps round to the start of the previous line:

```
┌─ LeftKeyAtStart ──────────────
│ ΔCursor
│ key?:    KEY
├───────────────────────────────
│ key? = left
│ column = 1
│ column' = numColumns
│ line > 1
│ line' = line – 1
└───────────────────────────────
```

Finally, a separate schema deals with the cursor being at the left of the top line. The cursor wraps round to the right of the bottom line:

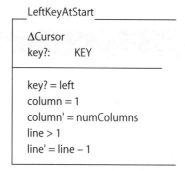

```
┌─ LeftKeyAtTop ────────────────
│ ΔCursor
│ key?:    KEY
├───────────────────────────────
│ key? = left
│ column = 1
│ column' = numColumns
│ line = 1
│ line' = numLines
└───────────────────────────────
```

These schemas can be combined to form one schema which defines the response of the cursor to a left-move key in all initial positions of the cursor.

LeftKey == LeftKeyNormal ∨ LeftKeyAtStart ∨
LeftKeyAtTop

4.   *NewDownKey*

NewDownKeyAtBottom
_____

ΔCursor
key?:   KEY
_____

key? = down
line = numLines
line' = numLines
column' = column
_____

NewDownKey ≙ DownKeyNormal ∨
NewDownKeyAtBottom

5.   *NewRightKey*

NewRightKeyAtRight
_____

ΔCursor
key?:   KEY
_____

key? = right
column = numColumns
column' = numColumns
line' = line
_____

NewRightKey == RightKeyNormal ∨
NewRightKeyAtRight

6.

(a)   Yes, the Prime Minister must be a Member
of Parliament because he or she is a
member of the Cabinet and the Cabinet is
a subset of the Members of Parliament.

(b)

HP
_____

MPs: ℙPERSON
Cabinet: ℙPERSON
DPM, PM: PERSON
_____

Cabinet ⊆ MPs
PM ∈ Cabinet
DPM ∈ Cabinet
DPM ≠ PM
_____

(c)   The new Prime Minister may not be the
same person as the old Prime Minister.

(d)   The new Prime Minister does not have to
be chosen from the Cabinet.

(e)   The outgoing Prime Minister does not
have to leave the Cabinet.

(f)   The outgoing Prime Minister may not
leave the Cabinet.

7.

(a)   The members of the new Cabinet must all
be MPs, to maintain the invariant that the
Cabinet is a subset of the MPs.

(b)   *ChangeCabinet2* requires a complete
change of personnel in the new Cabinet.

(c)   The error is that the PM is unchanged and
is always a member of the Cabinet, so the
Cabinet cannot change completely.

Chapter 7

1.

[PERSON]   the set of all uniquely identifiable persons

Computer
_____

users, loggedIn: ℙPERSON
_____

loggedIn ⊆ users
_____

InitComputer
_____

Computer'
_____

loggedIn' = ∅
users' = ∅
_____

RESPONSE ::=
OK | AlreadyAUser | NotAUser | LoggedIn | NotLoggedIn

2.   Add user

$AddUser_0$
_____

ΔComputer
p?:   PERSON
_____

p? ∉ users
users' = users ∪ {p?}
loggedIn' = loggedIn
_____

```
__ AddUserError _____
  ΞComputer
  p?:       PERSON
  reply!:    RESPONSE
  _____
  p? ∈ users
  reply! = AlreadyAUser
```

AddUser ==
(AddUser$_0$ ∧ [reply!: RESPONSE | reply! = OK]) ∨
AddUserError

3.

```
__ RemoveUser$_0$ _____
  ΔComputer
  p?:       PERSON
  _____
  p? ∈ users
  p ∉ loggedIn
  users' = users \ {p?}
  loggedIn' = loggedIn
```

```
__ RemoveUserError _____
  ΞComputer
  p?:       PERSON
  reply!:    RESPONSE
  _____
  (p? ∉ users ∧
  reply! = NotAUser)
  ∨
  (p? ∈ users ∧
  p? ∈ loggedIn ∧
  reply! = LoggedIn)
```

RemoveUser ==
(RemoveUser$_0$ ∧ [reply!: RESPONSE | reply! = OK]) ∨
RemoveUserError

4.   Log in

```
__ Login$_0$ _____
  ΔComputer
  p?:       PERSON
  _____
  p? ∈ users
  p? ∉ loggedIn
  loggedIn' = loggedIn ∪ {p?}
  users' = users
```

```
__ LoginError _____
  ΞComputer
  p?:       PERSON
  reply!:    RESPONSE
  _____
  (p? ∉ users ∧
  reply! = NotAUser)
  ∨
  (p? ∈ users ∧ p? ∈ loggedIn ∧
  reply! = LoggedIn)
```

Login ==
(Login$_0$ ∧ [reply!: RESPONSE | reply! = OK]) ∨ LoginError

5.   Log out

```
__ Logout$_0$ _____
  ΔComputer
  p?:       PERSON
  _____
  p? ∈ users
  p? ∈ loggedIn
  loggedIn' = loggedIn \ {p?}
  users' = users
```

```
LogoutError
┌─────────────────────────
│ ΞComputer
│ p?:       PERSON
│ reply!:   RESPONSE
├─────────────────────────
│ (p? ∉ users ∧
│ reply! = NotAUser)
│ ∨
│ (p? ∈ users ∧
│ p? ∉ loggedIn ∧
│ reply = NotLoggedIn)
└─────────────────────────
```

Logout ==
(Logout$_0$ ∧ [reply!: RESPONSE | reply! = OK]) ∨
LogoutError

Chapter 8

1.

loggedIn ⊆ users

2.

$\forall i: \mathbb{Z} \cdot i * i \geq 0$

3.

$\exists n: \mathbb{Z} \cdot n * n = n$

4.
{n: $\mathbb{N}$ | ($\forall$m: $\mathbb{N}$ | m ≠ 1 ∧ m ≠ n • n mod m ≠ 0) • n}

Chapter 9

1.

Latin: LANGUAGE
Latin ∉ ran speaks

2.

speaks ({Switzerland})= 4

3.

EU: ℙCOUNTRY
speaksInEU: COUNTRY ↔ LANGUAGE
speaksInEU = EU ◁ speaks

4.

grandParent: PERSON ↔ PERSON
grandParent = parent ; parent

5.
firstCousin: PERSON ↔ PERSON
firstCousin = (grandParent ; grandParent~) \ sibling

6.   Students are either from EU or overseas,
but not both. Students study and teachers teach.
Only offered modules can be studied. Those
modules that are taught are studied.

7.
studies ({p})

8.
#(teaches({p}))

9.   Inverse of *studies* relates modules to
persons studying them.

10.   The composition relates students to the
teachers who teach modules the students study.

11.
(studies ; teaches~)({p})

12.
#((studies ; teaches~)({p}) ∩ (studies ; teaches~)({q}))

13.
inter ◁ studies

14.
((teaches ; studies~))({p}) ∩ (teaches ;
studies~))({q})) ▷ inter ≠ ∅

15.
(a)
delegates ⊆ dom speaks
(b)
ran speaks ∩ official ≠ ∅
(c)
∃ lang: LANGUAGE •
  (∀del: PERSON | del ∈ delegates • del speaks lang)

(d)

∃ del: PERSON • del ∈ delegates •
  (∃ lang: LANGUAGE • del speaks lang ∧
  (∀otherDel: PERSON | otherDel ∈ delegates \ {del} •
      ¬(otherDel speaks lang)))

(e)

Register _____

del?:   PERSON
langs?: $\mathbb{P}$LANGUAGE
ΔCONFERENCE

---

del? $\notin$ delgates
delgates' = delegates $\cup$ {del?}
speaks' =
speaks $\cup$ {lan: LANGUAGE | lan $\in$ langs? $\cdot$ del? $\mapsto$ lan}
official' = official

Chapter 10

1.

(a) *bookedTo* is a function since it maps rooms to person and for any given room at most one person can book it. A person can book any number of rooms.

(b) The function is partial since not all rooms have been booked.

2.

▷ **Line 1:** gives the schema a name.
▷ **Line 2:** incorporates the schema $\Delta Hotel$; permits reference to state variables before and after this operation.
▷ **Line 3:** *p?* is an input variable – the person making the booking.
▷ **Line 4:** *r?* is an input variable – the room to be booked.
▷ **Line 5:** the room must not already be booked.
▷ **Line 6:** the maplet relating the room to the person is included in the new value of the function *bookedTo*.

3.

CancelBooking$_0$ _____

ΔHotel
p?:   PERSON
r?:   ROOM

{r? $\mapsto$ p?} $\in$ bookedTo
bookedTo' = bookedTo \ {r? $\mapsto$ p?}

4.

▷ **Line 1:** gives schema a name.
▷ **Line 2:** incorporates the schema $\Delta Hotel$; permits reference to state variables before and after this operation.
▷ **Line 3:** *p?* is an input variable – the person making the booking.
▷ **Line 4:** *r?* is an input variable – the room to be booked.
▷ **Line 5:** the room must already be booked to this person.
▷ **Line 6:** the maplet relating the room to the person is removed from the new value of the function *bookedTo*.

5.

(a) and (b)

Sydney2000 _____

participating: $\mathbb{P}$COUNTRY
events: $\mathbb{P}$EVENT
represents: PERSON $\rightarrowtail$ COUNTRY
competesIn: PERSON $\leftrightarrow$ EVENT
won: EVENT $\rightarrowtail$ PERSON

---

ran represents $\subseteq$ participating
$\forall$ ev: EVENT | ev $\in$ dom won $\cdot$ (won ev)
competesIn ev

▷ A person can only represent one country. An event has at most one winner.
▷ Persons may only represent participating countries. The person who wins an event must have been competing in it.

(c)

JoinGames _____

ΔSydney2000
c?:   COUNTRY

---

c? $\notin$ participating
participating' = participating $\cup$ {c?}
events' = events
represents' = represents
competesIn' = competesIn
won' = won

(d)

```
┌─ Win ─────────────────────────────
│ ΔSydney2000
│ p?:        PERSON
│ ev?:       EVENT
├───────────────────────────────────
│ ev? ∈ events
│ ev? ∉ dom won
│ p? competesIn ev?
│ won' = won ∪ {ev? ↦ p?}
│ participating' = participating
│ events' = events
│ represents' = represents
│ competesIn' = competesIn
└───────────────────────────────────
```

(e)

```
┌─ CountryGolds ────────────────────
│ ΞSydney2000
│ c?:         COUNTRY
│ golds!:   ℕ
├───────────────────────────────────
│ c? ∈ participating
│ golds! =
│    #{ev: EVENT | ev ∈ dom won ∧
│ won ; represents(ev) = c? • ev}
└───────────────────────────────────
```

Chapter 11

1.

```
┌─ SecureComputer ──────────────────
│ Computer
│ password:   PERSON ⇸ PASSWORD
├───────────────────────────────────
│ dom password = users
└───────────────────────────────────
```

2.

```
┌─ SecureInit ──────────────────────
│ SecureComputer
│ InitComputer
├───────────────────────────────────
│ password' = ∅
└───────────────────────────────────
```

3.

```
┌─ SecureAddUser₀ ──────────────────
│ AddUser₀
├───────────────────────────────────
│ password' = password ∪ {p? ↦ dummy}
└───────────────────────────────────
```

4.

```
┌─ SecureLogin₀ ────────────────────
│ ΔSecureComputer
│ Login
│ pwd?:    PASSWORD
├───────────────────────────────────
│ pwd? = password p?
└───────────────────────────────────
```

5.

```
┌─ ChangePassword₀ ─────────────────
│ ΔSecureComputer
│ Login
│ old?, new?:         PASSWORD
├───────────────────────────────────
│ p? ∈ loggedIn
│ password p? = old?
│ password' = password ⊕ {p? ↦ new?}
└───────────────────────────────────
```

Chapter 12

1.

u ⌢ v	=	⟨ London, Amsterdam, Madrid, Paris, Frankfurt ⟩
rev (u ⌢ v)	=	⟨ Frankfurt, Paris, Madrid, Amsterdam, London ⟩
rev u	=	⟨ Madrid, Amsterdam, London ⟩
rev v	=	⟨ Frankfurt, Paris ⟩
rev v ⌢ rev u	=	⟨ Frankfurt, Paris, Madrid, Amsterdam, London ⟩

2.

squash (2..4 ◁ rev (u ⌢ v)) = ⟨ Paris, Madrid, Amsterdam ⟩

3.

squash (4..2 ◁ rev (u ⌢ v)) = ⟨ ⟩

4.

$u \,\hat{}\, v \upharpoonright \{$ London, Moscow, Paris, Rome $\}$
$= \langle$ London, Paris $\rangle$

5.

tail $(u \,\hat{}\, v) \,\hat{}\,$ front $\langle$ Moscow, Berlin, Warsaw $\rangle$
$= \langle$ Amsterdam, Madrid, Paris, Frankfurt ,
Moscow, Berlin $\rangle$

6. The stream either consists of a sub-sequence before, then the pattern, then a sub-sequence after and *pos* is the index where the pattern starts, or it does not and *pos* is zero.

7.

```
┌─ Delete ─────────────────────────────
│ ΔTEXT
│ pat?:      seq CHAR
│ pos!:      ℕ
├──────────────────────────────────────
│ ((∃ before, after: seq CHAR • before ˆ pat? ˆ
│     after = stream) ∧ pos! = #before + 1 ∧
│     stream′ = before ˆ after)
│ ∨
│ (¬(∃ before, after: seq CHAR • before ˆ pat?
│     ˆ after = stream) ∧
│ pos! = 0 ∧ stream′ = stream)
└──────────────────────────────────────
```

Chapter 13

1.

```
┌─ FileSys ──────────────
│ file:     seq BYTE
│
└────────────────────────
```

2.

```
┌─ Init ──────────────────
│ ΔFileSys
├─────────────────────────
│ file′ = ⟨ ⟩
│
└─────────────────────────
```

3.

```
┌─ Insert ─────────────────────────────
│ ΔFileSys
│ pat?:      seq BYTE
│ pos!:      ℕ
├──────────────────────────────────────
│ 1 ≤ pos ≤ #file + 1
│ (∃ before, after: seq BYTE • before ˆ after =
│     file) ∧
│ pos! = #before + 1 ∧ file′ = before ˆ pat? ˆ
│     after)
└──────────────────────────────────────
```

4.

```
┌─ Delete ─────────────────────────────
│ ΔFileSys
│ beg?, end?:        ℕ
├──────────────────────────────────────
│ 1 ≤ beg? ≤ end? ≤ #file + 1
│ (∃ before, after, del: seq BYTE • before ˆ del ˆ
│     after = file) ∧
│ beg? = #before + 1 ∧ #del = end? − beg?
│ file′ = before ˆ after)
└──────────────────────────────────────
```

5.

```
┌─ Copy ───────────────────────────────
│ ΞFileSys
│ beg?, end?:        ℕ
│ buf!:              seq BYTE
├──────────────────────────────────────
│ 1 ≤ beg? ≤ end? ≤ #file + 1
│ (∃ before, after: seq BYTE • before ˆ buf! ˆ after =
│     file) ∧
│ beg? = #before + 1 ∧ #buf! = end? − beg?)
└──────────────────────────────────────
```

Chapter 14

1.

[APARTMENT, TIMESLOT, PERSON]

```
┌─ TimeShareCo ─────────────────────────────────
│ owned       ℙ APARTMENT
│ customers:  ℙ PERSON
│ booked:     APARTMENT ⇸ (TIMESLOT ⇸ PERSON)
├───────────────────────────────────────────────
│ dom booked = owned
│ ∀apart: APARTMENT | apart ∈ owned •
│ ran (booked a) ⊆ customers
└───────────────────────────────────────────────
```

```
┌─ Init ──────────────────────
│ ΔTimeShareCo
├─────────────────────────────
│ owned' = ∅
│ customers' = ∅
│ booked' = ∅
└─────────────────────────────
```

2.

```
┌─ AddCustomer ──────────────────────
│ ΔTimeShareCo
│ p? :       PERSON
├────────────────────────────────────
│ p? ∉ customers
│ customers' = customers ∪ {p?}
│ owned' = owned
│ booked' = booked
└────────────────────────────────────
```

3.

```
┌─ AddApartment ──────────────────────
│ ΔTimeShareCo
│ ap? :       APARTMENT
├─────────────────────────────────────
│ ap? ∉ owned
│ owned' = owned ∪ {ap?}
│ customers' = customers
│ booked' = booked ∪ {ap? ↦ ∅}
└─────────────────────────────────────
```

4.

```
┌─ MakeBooking ──────────────────────────────────────
│ ΔTimeShareCo
│ ap? :      APARTMENT
│ p? :       PERSON
│ t? :       TIMESLOT
├────────────────────────────────────────────────────
│ ap? ∈ owned
│ p? ∈ customers
│ t? ∉ dom (booked ap?)
│ booked' = booked ⊕ (ap? ↦ (booked ap? ∪ (t? ↦ p?)))
│ owned' = owned
└────────────────────────────────────────────────────
```

5.

```
┌─ FreeApartments ───────────────────────────────────
│ ΞTimeShareCo
│ t? :       TIMESLOT
│ free!:     ℙ APARTMENT
├────────────────────────────────────────────────────
│ ap? ∈ owned
│ free! = {apart: APARTMENT |
│ apart ∈ owned ∧ t? ∉ dom (booked apart) • apart}
└────────────────────────────────────────────────────
```

6.

(a)

- ▸ *position* maps an aircraft to its current position.
- ▸ *minsLeft* maps an aircraft to its remaining flying time (in minutes).
- ▸ *flightMins* maps each aircraft to a mapping that gives the time for the aircraft to fly to a given point (in minutes).

For each of the above the aircraft concerned are the REGA helicopters.

(b)

ran position ⊆ Switzerland

(c)

∀ch: POINT | inCH ∈ Switzerland •
(∃heli: AIRCRAFT | heli ∈ helis •
(flightMins heli) inCH ≤ 15)

(d)

ran position ⊆ ran base

(e)

position = base

(f)

$$\forall heli: AIRCRAFT \mid heli \in helis \bullet$$
$$(\exists basis: POINT \mid basis \in ran\ base \bullet$$
$$(flightMins\ heli)\ basis \leq minsLeft(heli))$$

Index